Illustrated Magic Dictionary

ILLUSTRATED MAGIC DICTIONARY

GEOFFREY LAMB

Drawings by Olga Lamb

ELSEVIER/NELSON BOOKS
New York

Library of Congress Cataloging in Publication Data

Lamb, Geoffrey Frederick.
   Illustrated magic dictionary.

   1. Conjuring—Dictionarie. I. Title.
GV1547.L28 1979   793.8'03   80-17050
ISBN 0-525-66689-3

Published in the United States by Elsevier/
Nelson Books, a division of Elsevier-
Dutton Publishing Company, Inc., New
York. Published simultaneously in Don
Mills, Ontario, by Nelson/Canada.

Printed in the U.S.A.   First U.S. Edition

10   9   8   7   6   5   4   3   2   1

CONTENTS

PREFACE

This book is intended particularly for the reader who is interested in magical entertainment but has no expert knowledge of the subject. It sets out to provide a fairly comprehensive guide to the magic scene, enabling him to find his way in a strange wonderland where nothing is quite what it seems.

Though compiled with the beginner especially in mind, the dictionary will, it is hoped, be useful also to the more experienced conjurer. Even the expert may find it convenient to have information brought together in a compact and handy form.

I have attempted to cover the whole field of magic as an entertainment in the belief that satisfying progress in magic can be made only by taking a wide view of the art, getting to know (for instance) a little of its history as well as some of its sleights and tricks. Thus the book deals with many aspects of conjuring: sleights, well-known tricks, technical terms, magic books, types of apparatus, and notable magical personalities.

A dictionary cannot be a text-book. While each entry, I hope, offers enough information to be helpful, long and detailed instructions would obviously be out of place. I have therefore given many references to books where such details may be discovered. In giving these I have borne in mind the likely availability in bookshops and libraries of books which may be helpful; for example, I have given numerous references to books currently available in paperback. Comparatively modern books predominate; thus Hugard appears far more often than Hoffmann. At the same time, for the sake of completeness, some references to a few older classics will be found.

These book references are not intended to be fully comprehensive (which would be outside the scope of this dictionary); they are merely suggestions, giving the beginner something to go on. As he continues with his magical reading he will no doubt jot down useful additions in the margin.

Magicians have inevitably provided a problem. There are literally hundreds of notable names in the history of magic past and present, and if this were a Who's Who many omitted names would have been included. But a selection obviously has to be made: the many whose names do appear are representative of the rest. An omission must not be regarded as a slight upon the magician concerned.

Time's winged chariot can be the enemy of any reference book. Names and addresses (e.g. of dealers) can become out of date in a couple of years. Very few addresses have therefore been given, for this is a dictionary and not a yearbook. Reference to current magical periodicals is the best way of keeping up to date with impermanent details.

The ideas and views expressed in the book are my own, but I am indebted to Peter Warlock for helping me to solve various problems, to Peter Lane for carefully checking dates of magical periodicals, and to Edwin Hooper, Goodliffe, Ron Macmillan, John Salisse, secretary of the Magic Circle, F. Alan Snowden, editor of THE MAGIC CIRCU-LAR, and George A. Jenness, for other help. Further acknowledgments will be found elsewhere.

GEOFFREY LAMB

Cross referencing by the use of italics has been included where it is felt that the reader might wish to refer to another entry for further information.

ACKNOWLEDGMENTS

For the illustrations to this book the author is particularly indebted to his wife, who drew the numerous very useful line drawings, and to Edwin Hooper for kindly providing many good and helpful photographs. He is also indebted to Derek Joseph for some excellent photographs of several items, and to various other kind people. Details showing illustration numbers are given below:

Edwin Hooper and the Supreme Magic Co.: 14, 15, 18, 21, 26, 27, 40, 41, 50, 51, 52, 55, 57, 58, 75, 79, 88, 89, 92, 105, 109, 120, 125, 137, 138, 139, 140.

Derek Joseph: 1, 42, 53, 57, 62, 66, 98, 131, 147, 148.

Hutchinson Publishing Group: 57, from *SECRETS OF MY MAGIC* by David Devant. (Reprinted by Supreme Magic Co.)

George A. Jenness: 98, from *MASKELYNE & COOKE.*

Alan Alan 63; Ali Bongo 102; Daily Mirror 52; Goodliffe 1, 78; Magic Circle 6, 66, 95, 96; Ron Macmillan 150; John Salisse 95, 96; F. Alan Snowden 83.

Saturday, 11th February, 1978   Vol. 65. No. 1672.

THE MAGIC CIRCLE

President
FRANCIS WHITE

Hon. Secretary:
JOHN SALISSE

Clubroom, Theatre, Museum
and Library
84 Chenies Mews.
London, W.C.1.
13th Feb: Ali Bongo Night.
20th Feb: From my Collection.
— Peter Lane

12p
30
CENTS

GOODLIFFE'S

ABRACADABRA

1672

The WORLD'S only MAGICAL WEEKLY

1. The world's only weekly magical journal.

A

Abracadabra. Old magic word of uncertain origin, freely used by modern conjurers. In earlier times it was believed to cure sickness, especially if written in triangular form, gradually diminishing:

```
A B R A C A D A B R A
  B R A C A D A B R
    R A C A D A B
      A C A D A
        C A D
          A
```

2. Harness worn under the dress, enabling assistant's body to be raised horizontally.

The name *ABRACADABRA* was adopted in February 1946 by *Goodliffe* as the title of the world's only weekly magical journal, which still flourishes after over 30 years. It circulates in 47 countries, and is almost indispensable to anyone who wishes to know what is happening in the magic world. It is published at Arden Forest Industrial Estate, Alcester, Warwickshire. *Illustration 1*. Donald Bevan is co-editor.

acquitment. Series of movements to show the hands apparently empty while an unseen article is secretly transferred to and fro between them.

act. Conjurer's complete performance, which may be anything from a 10-minute cabaret act to a full evening show.

Aerial Suspension. A trick derived from a feat performed by old Indian jugglers. The conjurer's assistant is supported by a stick under each armpit. One of the sticks is removed, and the assistant's body is then raised by the feet till he/she is in a horizontal position. A special harness worn under the dress (*illustration 2*) is the key to the mystery. *Robert-Houdin* made a feature of this trick, using his young son as assistant and pretending to administer ether to make the body as light as air! The trick is still performed very much in the same way, but a modern version, known as the Chair Suspension, has the girl lying on a board placed on the backs of two chairs. One of these is presently removed, leaving her suspended on the other; *illustration 37*. Sometimes the board is dispensed with. See Baron, *MAGIC SIMPLIFIED*, pp.96–7; Page,

BIG BOOK OF MAGIC, pp.290–1; Hoffmann, *MODERN MAGIC*, pp.495–501.

Aerial Treasury. Classic trick (also known as Miser's Dream, among other titles) in which the conjurer appears to snatch coin after coin from the air and drop them into a bucket, hat, or other receptacle. The coin that is caught has been *finger-palmed* or *back-palmed*. The performer pretends to drop it in the bucket but really palms it again. The coin which falls comes from a stack of coins in the other hand, which is holding the bucket. *Nelson Downs* presented a version of the trick which (with incidentals) was said to occupy about 30 minutes. See Hugard, *MODERN MAGIC MANUAL*, pp.62–70; Downs, *MODERN COIN MANIPULATION*.

Afghan Bands. An old trick in which large circular bands of paper (or cloth) are cut (or torn) lengthwise all the way round. The bands can be formed by cutting two-inch strips from an opened-out newspaper and sticking the ends together with sellotape. Normally, cutting a band in two will produce two separate bands half the width of the original. How-

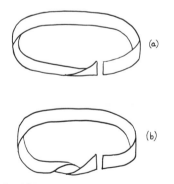

3. Afghan Bands given (*a*) half twist, (*b*) full twist.

ever, if a half-twist is given to the length of paper before the ends are joined, the result of cutting will be a single band twice the size of the original. If a full twist is given, the result will be two bands linked together; *illustration 3*. The origin of the title is obscure.

Aga illusion. *Levitation* feat. The performer 'hypnotizes' a lady assistant, placing her on a couch, and then causing her to rise in the air some three or four feet above the couch. The mechanism involves an upright rod protruding from the stage but hidden by the magician's body. There is also a horizontal arm on the end of which she rests; it can be cranked upward by a winch beneath the stage; *illustration 90*. Owing to the gooseneck shape of the arm (*illustration 91*) the performer is able to pass a hoop around her body. *Asrah*. See Gibson, *SECRETS OF THE GREAT MAGICIANS*, pp.110–12.

A.I.M.C. Associate of the Inner Magic Circle, an advanced degree of the famous magical society. *Magic Circle*.

Alan Alan. Lively professional magician, specializing in daring escapes, with many years of experience in theatre, cabaret, and circus; *illustration 63*. An experienced demonstrator and dealer, now with a shop at 88 Southampton Row, London.

Ali Bongo (William Wallace). Inventive professional magician, born in India but brought up in Kent; descended from his famous namesake, the thirteenth-century Scottish national leader. Well-known as adviser and assistant to the *David Nixon* TV magic shows, but also a splendid comedy conjurer in his own right, either as a breathless Arabian or in more ordinary dress; note *illustration 102*. His stage

name derives from a long-ago performance in a village pantomime.
American magicians. *Society of American Magicians*; *I.B.M.*

4. One of Professor Anderson's more modest posters. ('Magic', Jan. 1908, p. 27.)

Anderson, John Henry (1814–74). The most famous British conjurer of his day, usually known as Professor Anderson or the Wizard of the North. Born in Scotland, he first confined his youthful magical performances to his own country, but subsequently he performed successfully in England, America, and Australia. He was noted for his elaborate advertising methods (his posters proclaimed him 'The Wonder of the World' and for his use of showy apparatus, often made of solid silver. He was one of the first magicians to perform before Queen Victoria and the first British magician to entertain the Tsar of Russia. Two of the theatres he occupied were totally destroyed by fire: his own Theatre of Magic in Glasgow (1845) and Covent Garden Theatre, London (1856). His losses eventually bankrupted him. See *illustration 4*.

angle proof. Applied to a trick which can be performed without any secrets being visible to a spectator viewing the performance from a wide angle at the far side of the room or hall.

animals in magic. Many stage illusionists have used animals, from *rabbits* and *doves* to tigers and elephants, too often with little regard to the creatures' well-being. The use of animals provides the magician with many problems in addition to purely magical ones. Moreover, some members of an audience may strongly dislike seeing living creatures used as if they were inanimate objects. The beginner is strongly advised to concentrate on his own conjuring skill and to leave animals alone.

'Annals of Conjuring, The'. Title of a history of conjuring regarded as the standard work on the art up to the end of World War I. Written by Sidney W. Clarke, a lawyer by profession, it first appeared serially in the *MAGIC WAND* (1924–8). Only a few copies of it in book form were printed (1929).

Annemann, Theodore (1907–42). American *mentalist*, born Theodore John Squires; his mother was later Mrs Annemann. After quitting his job as railway clerk he joined a travelling medicine show as performer. Soon he began specializing in mental effects, appearing on his own as 'Annemann the Enigma'. Founded and edited the *JINX* magazine (1934), devoted to *mentalism*, and his influence in that field became widespread. At the early age of 35 he tragically committed suicide, from a variety of causes, including marital failures. His numerous books include *THE BOOK WITHOUT A NAME* (1931), *202 METHODS OF FORCING* (1933), and *PRACTICAL MENTAL EFFECTS* (1944), an outstanding book on the subject.

Any Card Called For. A startling effect in which the performer divides a shuffled pack into two, puts half in each trouser pocket, and invites the spectators to call out the names of any cards they please. As each card is named, the conjurer promptly pulls it from his pocket; *illustration 5*. The feat is accomplished by the use of *card indexes*; *illustration 28*.

5. Goldston's advertisement for 'Any Card Called For'.

apparatus. Visible object(s) used by a conjurer in his performance. Apparatus may be of any size, from a matchbox to a large cabinet. It may or may not be *faked*, but the more natural it looks the better. Beginners are advised to avoid gaudy apparatus that has obviously been made for nothing else but a conjuring trick, for spectators will naturally regard it with suspicion.

Artist's Dream, The. One of *Devant*'s earliest and most famous illusions, first produced at the *Egyptian Hall* in 1893. An artist's portrait comes to life, steps from the easel to embrace him while he sleeps, but vanishes when he wakes.

arithmetical magic. *mathematical magic.*

Asrah. *Levitation* illusion invented by *Servais Le Roy* c.1890, but still sometimes performed. A young lady is 'hypnotized' and placed on a table. A large cloth is placed over her, and presently she floats upward without any apparent means of support. A corner of the cloth is seized by the magician and whisked away. The lady has vanished. The trick is worked by a subtle substitution of a wire shape for the lady, but the deception is very hard to detect even if a spectator knows the secret.

assistant. Girl or man who openly helps the conjurer by bringing on needed apparatus, and sometimes by being levitated, vanished or produced from a cabinet, sawn in half, etc. *Robert-Houdin* used his young sons to assist him. There is an important difference between an assistant, who openly helps, and a *confederate*, whose help is secretly given. A helper from the audience is usually known to conjurers as a *volunteer.*

Atkins, Jeffery. For many years hon. treasurer of the *British Ring*, and one of the only two Englishmen to be elected president of the *I.B.M.* Notable for his 'Illusions of the Masters', regularly reviving feats of the famous old illusionists at British Ring conventions and similar functions. In private life director of a Southampton business.

audience participation. It is often desirable to get the whole audience involved in a trick instead of leaving them to be merely passive spectators. To take a simple example; if a card has been chosen by a spectator and its identity is to be revealed through apparent *thought-reading* by the performer, the whole audience (not just the one spectator) may be invited to concentrate on a mental picture of the card. They will thus all feel some sense of achievement when the performer at length succeeds in 'reading' the name of the card.

automata. Mechanical figures, very common in magical performances a hundred years and more ago, but rarely seen today except as curiosities. Among the most notable were two creations of *Robert-Houdin* – a writing figure (which could draw as well as write) and a performer on the trapeze – and four made by *Maskelyne*: *Psycho*, a companion figure named Zoe (which drew portraits of well-known people), and two musicians who played respectively the cornet and the euphonium; *illustration 6.*

MASKELYNE AND COOKE'S AUTOMATA AT THE EGYPTIAN HALL.

6. Four of Maskelyne's famous automata, with their creator. (Magic Circular, p.166.)

B

back-palm. Sleight (not for the beginner) in which an article, usually a card or coin, is surreptitiously transferred from the front of the hand to the back, so that the hand can be shown apparently empty. With a card the edges near the corner are gripped between the inside of the first and fourth fingers. A quick movement of the second and third fingers then swivels the card out of sight behind the hand; *illustrations 9, 10, 11.* A coin is back-palmed in somewhat similar fashion, the coin being balanced between first and fourth fingers as the second and third fingers double up and then straighten to come round in front of it; *illustrations 7, 8.* spider. See Hay, *AMATEUR MAGICIAN'S HANDBOOK*, pp.136-7. Delvin, *MAGIC OF THE MASTERS*, pp.22-7, 81-3.

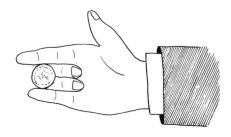

7. Back-palming a coin: middle fingers doubling up.

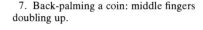

9. Back-palming a card: 1st stage, seen from front.

10. Back-palming a card: 2nd stage, seen from the front.

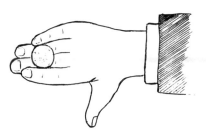

8. Coin back-palmed.

11. Back-palming a card: 3rd stage, seen from behind.

Baker, Roy. Vigorous and versatile British magician who has covered every type of magic act from theatre to house party. He specialized at one time in stage hypnotism, and is also an expert *mentalist*. But he has a flair for comedy, and is an experienced children's entertainer. Well-known as an inventor and dealer. Some of his best tricks are explained in *BAKER'S BONANZA* (1969, 1972) by Hugh Miller.

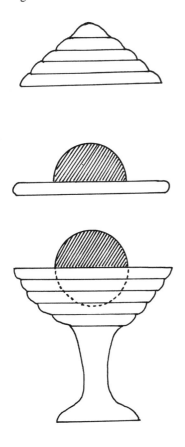

12. Ball Box, showing lid, fake, and ball in box.

Ball Box. Apparatus for making a small ball appear or vanish. It consists of a little wooden bowl on a pedestal, a lid, and a *fake* – a hollow shell which resembles the ball on one side and the interior of the lid on the other. It fits exactly into the lid, which appears empty when held towards the audience. A small ball is vanished; the lid of the box is lifted, leaving the fake resting on the bowl. This makes it seem that the ball has mysteriously entered the box. By replacing the lid and then lifting it in such a way that the fake is also raised, the pseudo-ball can be made to vanish. If the fake is now *palmed*, box and lid can be examined if anyone wishes. This is a very old trick but it is still found in some boxes of conjuring tricks. *Illustration 12.*

Ball of Wool Trick. A marked coin (or ring) is vanished and made to reappear in the centre of a ball of wool. The secret is a fairly flat tin tube, just big enough to receive the coin. The wool is previously wound into a ball around one end of the tube (*illustration 13*) and placed (for example) in the performer's pocket. Another coin is secretly substituted for the marked one, the latter being stealthily slipped into the tube, which is then withdrawn from the wool. The ball of wool is openly brought out and placed, say, in a glass tumbler. The substitute coin is vanished, and when a spectator unwinds the wool the marked coin is discovered within it. This is the oldest version of the trick. One modern version is to have the tube leading into the smallest of a *nest* of zip-fasten purses which can be closed in a single movement. See Devant, *THE BEST TRICKS*, pp.21–5; Dexter, *101 MAGIC SECRETS*, pp.132–3; Baron, *CLOSE-UP MAGIC FOR BEGINNERS*, pp.66–8.

17

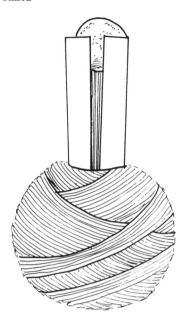

13. Ball of wool wound round flat tube.

14. Balloon penetrated with long needle.

balled. Rolled into a ball. A *silk* that has been tightly rolled up can be vanished by sleight-of-hand in the same way as a billiard ball, by the *French drop* or some other method. See Hugard, MODERN MAGIC MANUAL, pp.187–8.

balloon penetration. If a piece of sticky transparent tape is stuck on a blown-up balloon, a pin may be stuck into that spot without bursting the balloon. A dealer item is a long needle which, threaded with ribbon, may be pushed through an unfaked balloon; *illustration 14.*

balloons from hat. The production of fully inflated balloons makes an effective climax to a *hat production.* One method is a tablespoonful of bicarbonate of soda plus a little water in the balloon to be inflated, inside which is a smaller balloon containing tartaric acid, the neck tied with a bow knot which can quickly be undone by pulling one end of the thread.

Balls, Multiplying. *Billiard Balls.*

Bambergs, The. Famous Dutch family of magicians extending over six generations. First was Eliaser (1760–1833); then David (1786–1869); Tobias (1812–70); David Tobias (1843–1914), appointed to the royal court in 1870; and Theodore, famous as *Okito.* His son, David, became very popular in South America under the name *Fu Manchu.*

Basket Trick. Dramatic Indian illusion in which a child enters a round basket, through which a sword is then repeatedly thrust. The opening is smaller than the base, and although the basket appears only

18

just big enough to contain him, the child is able to curl his body around the inside of the base, leaving a space in the middle through which the magician thrusts his sword. Finally the child reappears in the basket, or else a double comes running in from behind the assembled spectators. In a European version popular last century the basket was oblong and the victim was a young lady. The trick was shown in its most dramatic form by *Stodare*, the thrusting of the sword through the basket (withdrawn apparently dripping with blood) being most realistic. In this case the basket, constructed on the lines of the *Inexhaustible Box*, was tipped forward and shown empty, the lady's double reappearing from the back of the theatre.

Beaufort, Douglas (Douglas Broad, 1864–1939). English magician who became a prominent Society entertainer after being sent down from Cambridge University and taking jobs as bank clerk, seaman, stage hand, and bill poster. He performed many times with *Maskelyne*. In the early 1890s he joined a British mission to Morocco as a magician. *NOTHING UP MY SLEEVE* (1938) is an entertaining autobiography.

Berglas, David. Outstanding British magician, successful in many countries on stage and TV, with earlier experience as P.T. instructor, musician, and hypnotist. He now specializes in *mentalism*, suggestion, table lifting, and similar apparent miracles, but he is also an accomplished conjurer in many fields. His one-man act is perhaps the nearest thing to the seemingly paranormal that can be seen on any stage, but he frankly disclaims any psychic powers.

Bertram, Charles (James Bassett, 1853–1907). The favourite performer of King Edward VII, and an able conjurer with a very genial manner. Although he sometimes gave public performances (e.g. with *Maskelyne and Cooke*) his reputation was even more strongly based on his popularity as a private entertainer at social functions. His jocular catchphrase 'Isn't it wonderful?' formed the title of his book of reminiscences and magical history (1896). An account of his travels was posthumously published (1911) under the title *A MAGICIAN IN MANY LANDS*.

bibliographies, conjuring. As there are literally thousands of books on conjuring and magic, a good bibliography can be very helpful. A very useful one is Robert Gill's *MAGIC AS A PERFORMING ART* (1976), which not only lists over 1,000 magic books published in English, mostly since 1935, but also gives details of each, including a brief comment. Trevor Hall's *BIBLIOGRAPHY OF BOOKS ON CONJURING IN ENGLISH FROM 1580 TO 1850* (1957) is an authoritative guide for those interested in the historical side; Edgar Heyl's *CONJURING BOOKS 1580–1850* (American, 1963) forms an appendix to it. R. Toole Stott's detailed *BIBLIOGRAPHY OF ENGLISH CONJURING 1581–1876* (1976) is also valuable and covers a slightly wider field. Clarke and Blind's *BIBLIOGRAPHY OF CONJURING AND KINDRED DECEPTIONS* (1920) is not confined to books in English but has long been out of print. *Findlay's NINTH COLLECTORS ANNUAL* (1975), a catalogue of his marvellous library, is in effect a wonderfully full bibliography covering every period, though regrettably it does not give names of publishers. Farelli's *MAGICAL BIBLIOGRAPHIES* (1953) is now virtually unobtainable.

Biff! Dramatic illusion originated by *Devant*. A motor-cyclist drove his machine into a raised packing-case. When a 'secret ray' was turned upon the case the roar of the cycle's engine ceased, the packing-case fell to pieces, and there was no sign of either cycle or cyclist. The illusion has recently been revived by Van Buren.

bill tube. Small metal tube with a secret inner part which has an opening near the bottom. The performer can secretly slip a marked banknote ('bill' U.S.A.) into this while the tube is in his pocket, and can then push the inner part home. As the tube has a cap or lid which is firmly fastened with a bolt, the appearance of the note in the tube (which can be casually examined) is most mysterious.

billet reading. A billet is a small piece of paper on which a spectator has written a word, a question, or a message. The billet is folded, or sealed in an envelope, but the performer succeeds in reading the writing. There are many methods, most of which involve either substitution of another piece of paper for the billet (which is read secretly), the doctoring of the envelope with alcohol to make it transparent, or the use of the *centre tear.*

Billiard Balls, Multiplying. Classic trick in which a billiard ball is produced from nowhere, and then further balls appear one at a time between all the fingers of one hand, sometimes of both hands. There are many variations; golf balls are sometimes used; *illustration 5.* The secret is a half *shell* exactly resembling the ball over which it is placed. The latter is rolled out from behind the shell with one finger, thus making one ball apparently change into two. A similar process is repeated until the hand holds four balls. For reference see Hugard, *MODERN MAGIC MANUAL*, pp.121–8; 135–7; Elliott, *CLASSIC SECRETS OF MAGIC*, pp.124–41.

Bird-Cage, Vanishing. Trick invented by *De Kolta*, in which a bird-cage containing a canary vanishes while held in the performer's hands. The cage folds into a small compass and is drawn up the performer's sleeve by a *pull*. At its worst this is a nauseating trick made notorious by *Carl Hertz*, who, in spite of his pretence to the contrary, freely dumped dead canaries in the dustbin after his shows. If the bird is a live one it can hardly escape from being injured or killed. The few performers who still do this trick generally use a dummy bird, but if this is sufficiently lifelike to deceive people, intelligent and sensitive members of the audience will none the less be unhappy. It is a trick best avoided unless the cage is obviously empty. *Illustrations 16, 17.*

biseauté cards. *stripper* cards.

Bishop, Washington Irving (1856–89). Perhaps the first man to popularize *muscle-reading* as a special form of so-called mind-reading. Bishop was an eccentric American who began by combining mind-reading with Spiritualist exposures, but claimed supernormal powers himself. From childhood he was subject to cataleptic fits, and his death at the early age of 33 was the subject of furious controversy. After performing one of his favourite tricks at a social club he suddenly collapsed. He was thought to be dead, and an autopsy was carried out a few hours later by a doctor anxious to study his brain. His mother subsequently accused the doctor of murdering her son, who would, she maintained, have recovered from his fit if left to himself.

Black Art. Important magical principle based on the fact that black against black is virtually invisible. A black thread may be used to make an article move mysteriously. The conjurer's table, moreover, is sometimes covered with black cloth and fitted with one or more holes (known as wells) also lined with black cloth and therefore almost invisible. These are used for vanishing small articles. The fullest development of the principle is a full-scale stage performance with a background of black curtains. Bright lights directed towards the audience help to make persons clothed and masked in black completely invisible on the stage. They can thus make furniture and other objects apparently move about of their own accord. A bodiless head and a headless body can be similarly contrived. An ingenious person can devise numberless similar mysteries. *Black Light.*

Black Light. Ultra-violet light shining on articles coated with fluorescent paint and producing a brilliant glow, particularly useful in *Black Art* shows.

Blackstone, Harry (Henri Bouton, 1885–1965). For many years America's leading magician, after the death of *Thurston*. Starting his career as a cabinet-maker, he began constructing equipment for a magic dealer, and then decided to become a performer. His first appearances were with his brother (a clown) in a vaudeville act. Later he presented

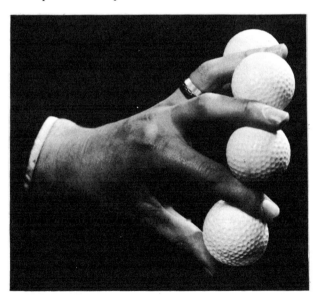

15. Multiplying golf balls.

Blendo

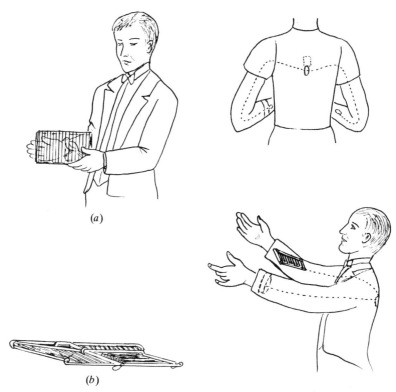

16. The Vanishing Bird-cage, (a) opened out, (b) collapsed.

17. How the bird-cage passes up the performer's sleeve.

himself as 'Fredrik the Great', but during World War I he changed this German name to Blackstone, and under this name until his retirement he presented a very big illusion show with numerous assistants, mostly glamorous girls, calling it 'The Show of a Thousand and One Wonders'. Though featuring many large illusions, such as The Vanishing Horse, and *Sawing a Woman in Half*, he was equally notable for his masterly handling of the *Dancing Handker-*

chief. The books written under his name were in fact compiled by *Walter B. Gibson.*

Blendo. In its original form three silks, red, white, and blue respectively, changed suddenly to a Union Jack. The flag was carefully folded and concealed behind the silks, which were afterwards drawn inside the flag (a double one). Nowadays a big rainbow silk often takes the place of a flag.

blindfold. To bandage a magician's

eyes with even a large handkerchief does not normally deprive him completely of sight. By lowering his eyebrows as the bandage is tied, and by subsequently raising them, he can see down the sides of his nose sufficiently to recognize articles on a table close to him. He should, however, be careful to act as if he cannot see at all. It is possible to see to some extent through a large dark-coloured silk *foulard* that is rolled up on two opposite sides. A slight gap between the rolls enables the performer to have some vision through a single layer of silk. The audience, of course, must be given the impression that the bandage is quite a thick one. Pads of cotton wool or lumps of dough are sometimes placed on the eyes before bandaging, but these are also raised slightly by eyebrow movement or pushed up in the process of putting a (faked) black bag over the head. See Dexter, *SEALED VISION*; Joseph, *INTUITIONAL SIGHT*.

Blindfold Drive. Publicity effect wherein the performer, heavily blindfolded and usually with a bag over his head, drives a car through the streets. There are various methods by which he contrives to see, despite the apparently effective way of sealing his vision. See Dexter, *SEALED VISION*.

Blitz, Antonio (1810–77). Popular European magician, possibly English, though he claimed to be German. He settled in America in 1835 and established a great reputation there. His particular aim was to amuse and entertain his audiences as well as mystify them. A great many imitators took his name, and it is sometimes difficult to know, in written records, which Blitz is really being referred to. In 1871 he wrote *FIFTY YEARS IN THE MAGIC CIRCLE*, a lively account of his conjuring experiences.

body load. *Load* concealed on the performer's body, often under cover of the jacket.

Book Test. Popular type of *mentalism* trick wherein one or more spectators help to choose a word in a given (or selected) book and the performer succeeds in discovering the word without looking in the book. There are many versions of the trick, in most of which the word is forced in one way or another. Sometimes a whole line is 'read'. See Hugard, *MODERN MAGIC MANUAL*, pp.318–20; Elliott, *MAGIC: 100 NEW TRICKS*, pp.188–91; Adair, *MENTAL MAGIC*, pp.39–40.

books, conjuring. Books issued by general publishers (e.g. Kaye & Ward, Faber, David & Charles) should be obtainable through any bookseller. The books of magical publishers (e.g. Supreme Magic, Goodliffe, Hades) are normally obtainable only through magic dealers who handle books, such as *Davenports* or Magic Books by Post (29 Hill Avenue, Bedminster, Bristol). This is a limited and specialized trade and so a stamped addressed envelope should usually be enclosed when asking for lists. Supreme and Goodliffe each supply mainly their own publications. Second-hand magic books are not often found on the shelves of ordinary second-hand booksellers but can be obtained from Elizabeth McMillan (1 Bellevue Road, Kirkintilloch, Glasgow) and occasionally from other advertisers in *ABRACADABRA*. *Illustration 18.*

borrowing. Conjurers traditionally borrow small articles such as coins, rings, and handkerchiefs to use in

18. Bookstall at a magic convention.

their tricks, as implied proof that these articles are free from trickery. Comedy may also be obtained by apparently subjecting the article to deliberate or accidental ill-treatment. Any such article should of course be returned in the same condition in which it was received, or if a Treasury note, for instance, has been torn or crumpled, it should be replaced by one in good condition. Breaches of this rule are apt to bring conjuring into disrepute. There is a good case (on hygienic grounds) for *not* borrowing handkerchiefs. Though borrowing has its place in magic, especially with a small audience, it is better for a conjurer to use his own article than to hinder the flow of his performance by laboriously trying to coax the desired article out of a large or reluctant audience.

Bosco, Bartolomeo (1790–1863). Showy Italian conjurer who performed in many countries and spoke many languages, with a marked Italian accent. He dressed flamboyantly and made an impressive appearance on the stage, but his best trick was apparently the old fairground *Cups and Balls*. In his *MEMOIRS* Robert-Houdin has given a vivid picture of Bosco's style of performance, notable among other things for an exceptionally callous treatment of livestock. Another contemporary speaks of him as 'that distasteful fat old Italian'.

Botania. An empty flower-pot is covered with a tube also shown empty. When the tube is removed a large flower-bush is seen in the pot. Compressible feather flowers are placed around an inner lining, which leaves the tube looking empty. The pot has catches which grip the lining, this being hidden as the flowers

expand. *Bouquet, magic*; *Mango Tree Trick.*

Bottle and Glass Trick. An old trick also known (not very suitably) as the *Passe-Passe Trick*. A bottle and a glass are each concealed by a cardboard tube and made to change places; *illustrations 19, 20*. There are in fact a glass tumbler and a bottomless bottle-shell within each tube. With pressure on the tube the shell is lifted, leaving the glass exposed, so that the conjurer can reveal either the bottle or the glass at will. A modern embellishment is to have several bottle-shells fitting together, thereby enabling the number of bottles to increase, usually to the apparent confusion of the magician. This often causes amusement, but it perhaps gives away part of the secret. See Hoffmann, *MODERN MAGIC*, pp.435–6; Delvin, *MAGIC OF THE MASTERS*, p.198.

Bottle Imp. Miniature bottle weighted at the base so that it will not lie horizontal when a spectator tries to make it do so, though it will meekly lie on its side when the performer commands. The top of the bottle is hollow, and he secretly inserts a small nail, thereby weighting the top.

Bottle, Inexhaustible. *Inexhaustible Bottle.*

bottom card. The card at the bottom when the pack is face down. It is usually still regarded as the bottom card even if the pack is turned face up.

bottom deal. A sleight employed when the performer wishes to substitute secretly the bottom card for one of the cards he is dealing in the normal way from the top. The thumb and fingers of the right hand (dealing) seem to take the top card but really seize the bottom card,

25

19. Bottle and glass.

20. Bottle and glass transposed.

which has been slightly pushed forward by a finger of the left hand. The move should be imperceptible, but it needs practice to perform it smoothly. The sleight can be used as a *force*. A spectator is asked to give a number. The card to be forced is at the bottom of the pack, and is substituted for the card at the chosen number.

bottomless glass. Glass or plastic tumbler with the bottom removed, preferably leaving a small rim. If this is covered with a disc the tumbler can be used normally. Useful in connection with *palming* for vanishing or producing a small article, the tumbler often first being covered with a handkerchief.

bouquet, magic. A favourite trick of many conjurers is to produce one or more bouquets of what they hope the audience will regard as flowers. The 'flowers', however, are sometimes all too obviously artificial and easily compressible (they are made of dyed feathers). These produc-

tions are usually drawn from the sleeve, from hidden compartments in a large shawl, or from within a tube. Perhaps their main virtue is that they are showy and colourful. *Illustration 21.*

box the cards. Cut the pack into two halves which are brought face to face, with backs showing at both top and bottom.

Box Trick. Illusion in which the performer or his assistant is shut up in a large box or trunk, which is then locked and roped, but from which he succeeds in escaping when the box is hidden by a screen. Although many ways of *faking* the box are known, such as a concealed trap in one end, the secret is sometimes so cleverly disguised that the box can be examined by a committee from the audience. The first to introduce the Box Trick were probably *Maskelyne and Cooke*, though *Lynn* disputed this. Subsequent performers sometimes added embellishments, such as *Houdini*'s escape from a

26

21. Production of a bouquet from a foulard by Ian Adair.

packing-case nailed together on the spot, and his escape from a box lowered under water. Maskelyne used to offer a challenge with a reward of £500 to anyone who could duplicate his famous box. In 1898 the challenge was taken up by two young men, and although the secret of their box was probably different from his own, his refusal to disclose his secret lost him the legal case which ensued. *Substitution Trunk.*

Brainwave Pack. A pack of cards *faked* in such a way that when a spectator names any card, the performer at once removes the pack from its case and shows that the named card is the only one face up. Moreover, the same card has a back that is different from all the others. This apparent miracle is worked by an ingenious use of the *rough-and-smooth principle.* The effect is so remarkable that perhaps the greatest difficulty lies in convincing the audience that the spectator is not a *confederate.* See Gibson, *COMPLETE ILLUSTRATED BOOK OF CARD MAGIC,* pp.351–3.

break. Gap between two sections of a pack of cards, usually maintained by the tip of the little finger.

breakaway. Term applied to a wand or fan which collapses when a spectator tries to use it. The wand becomes limp and the fan appears to be broken, though both articles can be used normally if the conjurer desires. They can be obtained from magic dealers.

Brewster, Sir David (1781–1868). Distinguished scientist, whose *LETTERS ON NATURAL MAGIC* (1832) show how easily man's senses can be deceived by optical illusions, strange acoustic effects, and mechanical automata; they deal also with some curiosities of fire endurance.

bridge. Curved gap between two halves of a pack of cards, caused by secretly squeezing the ends of the top half downward and the ends of the lower half upward. The cards can be cut at the bridge by sense of touch; *illustration 22.*

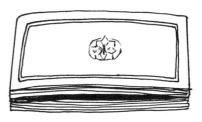

22. Bridged pack of cards.

27

British Magical Society. The oldest magic club in Britain. *Societies, magical.*

British Ring. Section of the *I.B.M.*, the 25th to be founded (1928), and the largest of the many Rings. Two of its members have been International Presidents of the I.B.M., the only non-Americans to hold the office. The Ring usually holds three or four meetings each year, including a big five-day convention, widely attended. A monthly journal, *THE BUDGET*, is published. *Atkins; Strickland.*

Brooke, Ken. A leading magic demonstrator and close-up performer. Originally from Yorkshire, he joined *Harry Stanley*'s magic business in 1962. Later he set up his own magic showroom in London's West End, known as Ken Brooke's Magic Place, a rendezvous for many distinguished magicians.

Buckingham, Geoffrey. One of the great sleight-of-hand performers, whose manipulative act with coins, balls, and thimbles has long been world-famous. His book *IT'S EASIER THAN YOU THINK* (1952) is a classic of manipulative magic.

buckle. To squeeze one or more cards at the bottom of a pack or *packet*, causing it (them) to buckle up under the rest and remain out of sight of the audience.

buckle count. Holding one or more cards buckled and thus hidden while counting the visible cards. *False count.*

Bullet Catch. A trick with a long and sometimes fatal history. It was featured safely and successfully by *Anderson, Blitz*, and *Alexander Herrmann*, among others, but *Houdini*, bold as he was, refused to risk it. The danger from carelessness or malevolence has been very real. An Indian juggler (1818) and the wife of a Polish conjurer named Linski (1820) were both fatally shot when facing the gun. Later in the century Dr Epstein was killed by the end of his ramrod, which broke off inside the pistol barrel. In 1899 a Hungarian performer named Hatal died through momentary carelessness in preparing the gun, and the same lapse led to the death of Herr Blumenfeld (1906). The most famous victim of all was *Chung Ling Soo* (1918). Other performers of the feat have suffered serious facial injuries. In spite of its grim history the trick is still sometimes performed by bold and confident magicians.

C

Cagliostro, Count Alessandro di (1743–95). Magical impostor, probably Giuseppe Balsamo, but whose true career is uncertain and mysterious, depending mainly on biased records. He assumed the title of Count, toured Europe, founded an Egyptian order of Freemasonry, and practised alchemy, before being seized by the Church. Magicians sometimes use his well-known name to lend colour to certain tricks. See Robert-Houdin, *MEMOIRS*, Chap. 16.

Cake Baked in a Hat. Popular nineteenth-century trick. Flour, water, etc. were mixed up and poured into a borrowed top hat; *illustration 23*. Actually they went into a round tin which had been secretly *loaded* (together with a cake) into the hat. A larger tin containing the cake mixture was casually lowered into the hat, bringing away with it the smaller tin and leaving the cake behind; *illustration 24*. 'Heating' over a candle was usual – and occasionally disastrous. See Robert-Houdin, *MEMOIRS*, Chap. 7.

Calvert, John. American illusionist, formerly a film star, who presents perhaps the largest magic show of the day under the title 'Magicarama'. He takes his show around the world in a large yacht named 'The Magic Castle', which was unfortunately wrecked in 1977. The special feature of his act is an electric organ which floats out over the footlights and orchestra pit. Following Blackstone, he also offers

23. Cake mixture poured into hat.

24. The two cake tins, lower one showing space for cake. Note springs at side to grip upper tin.

29

25. Card box, showing flap.

a brilliant *Dancing Handkerchief* routine.

Cane, Dancing. *Dancing Cane.*

card box. Small box with a loose flap which fits either the hinged lid or the bottom of the box; *illustration 25*. If a card is previously placed secretly between the flap and the lid, and a different card is placed openly in the box, a change of card is effected when the box is closed and the flap falls from the lid to the bottom. A card can be vanished or produced by a similar use of the box. However, if such apparatus is used at all it should be used both sparingly and unobtrusively. It should be treated as if it were merely a box for holding a pack of cards and not as a piece of conjuring apparatus. Another (metal) form of box has a hinged flap which locks in position and can be handled by a spectator, but it will take only one or two cards.

card change. The secret substitution of one card for another, the former usually being the top card of the pack. The pack is held in the left hand, the card to be changed in the right. The latter is slipped by the

second and third fingers under the bottom of the pack while the thumb and first finger quietly remove the top card. The movement of the hands coming together is disguised by a turn of the body to the left as the card is apparently just placed on the table. Various other forms of change are also employed. *Flap card*; *Mexican turnover*. See Gibson, COMPLETE ILLUSTRATED BOOK OF CARD MAGIC, pp.105–23.

card discovery. The revelation of a chosen card in some magical way. For example, the performer may throw the cards in the air and pretend to snatch the chosen card from the rest, or cause it to be reversed in the pack, or make it appear at a chosen number. *rising cards*; *card sword*. Various methods of card discovery will be found in most books on card tricks, e.g. Baron, CARD TRICKS FOR BEGINNERS; Lamb, YOUR BOOK OF CARD TRICKS; Hugard, ENCYCLOPEDIA OF CARD TRICKS.

card fan. To *fan* a pack or group of cards is to spread them in the hand in semi-circular form, resembling a fan. This is often done to show that the cards are mixed. But it may also be done as a sleight, one or more fans of cards being magically produced (by *back-palming*) from behind the elbow, etc. Card fanning with the backs of the cards to the audience is often performed as a *flourish*, different coloured backs producing various attractive patterns. A giant fan has two banks of cards interlaced; *illustration 26*. Often the fan is extended to form a complete circle; *illustration 27*. See Gibson, COMPLETE ILLUSTRATED BOOK OF CARD MAGIC, pp.250–74. *reversed fan*.

card flourish. Jugglery with the cards,

26. Giant card fan.

27. Giant circular fan shown by Lewis Ganson.

such as *springing* them from hand to hand, *spreading* them along the arm, or *fanning* them. See Gibson, COM-PLETE ILLUSTRATED BOOK OF CARD TRICKS, pp.237–75.

card force. Secret method of compelling a spectator to take the card the performer wishes, though ostensibly a free choice is offered. The standard force is to run the cards from hand to hand and to push forward the desired card just as the spectator's fingers approach the cards. An alternative device is the *knife force*, and there are many other methods of forcing. *Bottom deal*; *forcing pack*. See Gibson, COM-PLETE ILLUSTRATED BOOK OF CARD MAGIC, pp.161–71; Clive, CARD TRICKS WITHOUT SKILL, pp.31–4.

card frame. Small picture frame which is shown apparently empty and in which a forced card then mysteriously appears. The card is already in the frame, hidden by a piece of black cloth (ostensibly the back of the frame) just inside the glass. Before vanishing a duplicate the performer covers the frame with a large handkerchief. In removing this he also removes the cloth, leaving the card visible. Alternatively a *sand frame* may be used.

Card in Cigarette. Trick in which a card is torn up and the pieces placed in an envelope or *card box*, after which the performer borrows a cigarette. It refuses to draw when he lights it, so he tears it open and finds the selected card, now restored. The envelope or card box contains only some shreds of tobacco. There are many variations, including a Card in a Packet of Chewing-gum, a speciality of *Roy Johnson*. See Devant, THE BEST TRICKS, pp.63–5; Johnson, THE ROY JOHNSON EXPERIENCE, pp.71–6.

31

28. Card index.

card index. A flat, double-sided container with numerous pockets; *illustration 28*. Each side has enough pockets to allow all the cards from one suit to be arranged in regular order, with one or more cards in each pocket. Two card indexes will accommodate the whole pack. With one index in each pocket the conjurer can perform *Any Card Called For*. Indexes can be obtained from dealers or made at home from cardboard. (Note that 'indexes' is the

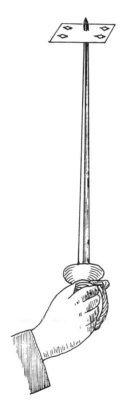

29. Card sword.

30. Hilt of card sword, showing hidden card.

31. Tip of card sword.

correct plural; 'indices' has a mathematical connection.)

card location. Any secret method of finding a chosen card that has been returned to the pack and *lost*: e.g. *crimping* a corner or using a *key card*.

card stab. Dramatic form of card discovery. A chosen card, apparently *lost* in the pack but actually kept in view by the performer (e.g. an *upside-down card* in a *one-way* pack), is stabbed with a knife or dagger when the cards are spread face down on the table, even though the performer may be *blindfold*. There are various ways of performing the trick. Sometimes the pack, wrapped in paper, is stabbed from the side, and the knife is found to be touching the chosen card. See Clive, CARD TRICKS WITHOUT SKILL, p.130; Reed, MAGICAL MIRACLES YOU CAN DO, pp.28–9.

card sword. Apparatus for revealing a chosen card shuffled into the pack. The cards are tossed into the air and a thrust made at them with the sword, which is seen to have picked out and pierced the chosen card. The latter was in fact *forced*, and a duplicate was inserted in a special holder in the hilt, attached to a piece of elastic which draws it to the tip of the sword; *illustrations 29, 30, 31. card stab*. See Hoffmann, MODERN MAGIC, pp.121–5; Page, BIG BOOK OF MAGIC, pp.97–9.

card through handkerchief. Classic form of *card discovery*. The pack is wrapped in a handkerchief and shaken, whereupon the chosen card appears to penetrate the handkerchief; *illustration 32*. The card is really wrapped in an outside fold of the handkerchief; *illustration 33*. Either it is brought to the top of the pack and palmed before wrapping,

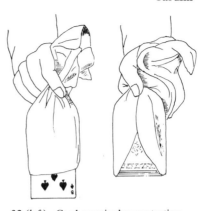

32 (*left*). Card seemingly penetrating handkerchief.

33 (*right*). Card in fold of handkerchief.

or else a duplicate of a *forced* card is palmed. See Hugard, MODERN MAGIC MANUAL, p.359; Stanyon, CONJURING WITH CARDS, pp.25–6; Elliott, CLASSIC SECRETS OF MAGIC, pp.18–22 (novel method); Clive, CARD TRICKS WITHOUT SKILL, pp.131–2.

cardician. Sleight-of-hand performer with playing-cards.

Cardini (Richard Pitchford, 1899–1973). Welsh-born conjurer who performed one of the best and most famous of all sleight-of-hand acts. At one time a salesman in *Gamage*'s conjuring department, he went to America in 1926, where he developed a routine in which he came on stage as a slightly inebriated man-about-town to whom strange things happened. Fans of cards, lighted cigarettes, and billiard balls kept appearing in his fingers, to his apparent confusion. This type of silent act was often copied, but no other performer has ever reached Cardini's excellence. *Dai Vernon*, one of the greatest magical perfectionists, considered that Cardini's act was flawless.

Cards Across. Classic trick known by various names. Several cards are counted and given to a spectator to hold. Another batch of cards, also counted, is handed to a second spectator. Three or four cards are now made to pass mysteriously from one spectator to the other. Many different methods have been worked out, most of them involving some sleight-of-hand. An easier but ingenious one is described in Baron, CARD TRICKS FOR BEGINNERS, pp.100–4. See also Gibson, COMPLETE ILLUSTRATED BOOK OF CARD TRICKS, pp.215–20; Hay, AMATEUR MAGICIAN'S HANDBOOK, pp.101–3;

Hugard and Braue, ROYAL ROAD TO CARD MAGIC, pp.289–92.

Cards to Pocket. Trick in which ten cards seemingly pass up the performer's sleeve and down into his trouser pocket, the transposition being performed bit by bit. The feat is accomplished by bold and skilful palming. See Hugard, MODERN MAGIC MANUAL, pp.354–7. Gibson, COMPLETE ILLUSTRATED BOOK OF CARD TRICKS, pp.211–15; Hay, AMATEUR MAGICIAN'S HANDBOOK, pp.95–8; Hugard and Braue, ROYAL ROAD TO CARD MAGIC, pp.279–87.

Carmo, The Great (Harry Cameron, 1881–1944). Australian-born magi-

34. Witch's cauldron, showing birds packed into lid.

35. Inner part of lid left in cauldron as birds escape.

cian who settled in England. Performed for a time with Le Roy, but was best known for the big Carmo Circus which mixed illusions, dancers, animal acts, etc. under canvas. He was often dogged by ill fortune and suffered serious financial losses.

Carter, Charles Joseph (1874–1936). American magician often known as Carter the Great, better known in the East than in his own country. The bulk of his time was spent in world tours. He presented a lavish show and achieved great success with it, but lost money when he opened a theatre of magic in the U.S.A.

Cauldron, The Witch's. Stage illusion common in Victorian times and even later. Pails of water were poured into a cauldron and some eggs were dropped inside. The lid was placed on, a fire lit beneath, and in due course several pigeons and/or ducks flew out, sometimes the worse for wear. The secret was that they had been cooped up inside the lid, which was fashioned after the style of the *dove pan* lid. One of those tricks better neglected than performed. *Illustrations 34, 35.*

centre tear. A spectator writes a word

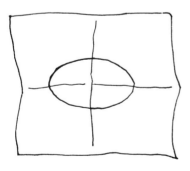

36. Centre tear: word written in oval, paper folded as shown by lines.

in the middle of a *billet*, which he then folds twice; *illustration 36*. The performer tears the billet up and usually sets fire to it. But he *steals* the folded centre and secretly reads it under cover of the slate or writing-pad on which he is proposing to write the word when he has 'read' the spectator's mind. See Hugard, *MODERN MAGIC MANUAL*, pp.310–12; Elliott, *MAGIC AS A HOBBY*, pp.182–5; Adair, *CONJURING AS A CRAFT*, pp.136–9.

Chair Suspension. *Aerial Suspension*; *illustration 37.*

changing bag. A small cloth bag mounted on a wooden handle which is attached to a ring around the open mouth of the bag; *illustration 38*. The bag may be turned inside out and shown empty, but there is a false lining. A turn of the handle can bring this lining from one side of the bag to the other, and thus an examined article placed in the bag can be secretly exchanged for a *faked* one. Similarly a batch of cards bearing different names can be *switched* for a batch all bearing a name that the performer wishes to *force*. A plausible reason for using the bag should always be found (e.g. to ensure that the performer does not touch the article). A faked paper bag (divided down the middle) may be used as a changing bag.

Chapender, Martin (H. M. Jones, c.1876–1905). Polished English magician making a great reputation for himself, especially as a billiard ball manipulator, when he died from meningitis before the age of 30. The *Magic Circle* was formed partly as a memorial to him, and its chief founder, Neil Weaver, at first intended calling it the Martin Chapender Club.

Charlier pass. One-handed *pass* (or

35

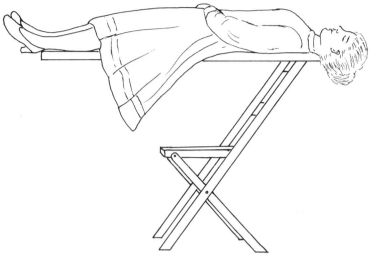

37. Chair suspension.

38. Changing bag.

cut) with cards (*illustration 39*), named after a mysterious French amateur of the mid-Victorian period who displayed wonderful dexterity in handling cards. He lived for a time in England and is described by *Bertram* in *ISN'T IT WONDERFUL?* (pp.109–15) and *Hoffmann* in *CONJURER DICK* (Chap. 15). See Gibson, *COMPLETE ILLUSTRATED BOOK OF CARD MAGIC*, pp.82–7; Hugard and Braue, *ROYAL ROAD TO CARD MAGIC*, pp.184–5.

Charlton, Christopher H. (1883–1963). One of the most accomplished English magicians of the Edward VII–George V period. Though less flamboyant than some contemporaries (he did not carry tons of apparatus), he presented an act that has been called 'the ideal vaudeville magic offering'. He never used living creatures in his entertainment. His fine collection of magic books and periodicals is now in the Magic Circle reference library.

Chess Player. Eighteenth-century automaton constructed by an Austro–Hungarian nobleman, Baron von Kempelen. It was a life-size figure of a Turk seated on a cabinet filled with complicated machinery. This was wound up before the exhibition began, and the

39. Charlier pass: top half of pack raised by thumb, lower half replacing former top half.

Turk would then play a game of chess with any opponent, nearly always winning. Spectators were bewildered by the automaton's skill, but the secret was simple. The machinery was sheer misdirection: a living person (an excellent chess player) was concealed within the cabinet, avoiding detection by a series of subtle moves when the doors were opened. The figure was sold to America and was destroyed in a fire in 1854.

children's magic. Performing magic for children is a specialized art which cannot adequately be summarized in a few words. Desirable, at least, is a liking for children and an ability to see things from their point of view without losing their respect. Sucker gags, noisy audience participation, the introduction of a rabbit, and so on, though quite common are by no means essential. Fun and laughter must be present, but preferably blended with genuine mystery. Some useful books on children's magic are: Eric Lewis and Wilfred Tyler, *OPEN SESAME* (1947, 1968); Wilfred Tyler, *PLAYING WITH MAGIC* (1953); John Brearly, *CON-JUNIORING* (1945); Peter D'Arcy, *CHILDREN'S PARTIES A SPECIALITY* (1972).

Chinese magic. Popular style of conjuring based on real Chinese tricks, the *Linking Rings* and the *Goldfish Bowls* being the best known. The first Chinese magicians to visit Europe appeared in Britain about 1830 and greatly influenced *Phillippe*. The showy robes worn by these and later Chinese conjurers such as *Ching Ling Foo* have attracted several Western performers, who have either featured a completely Chinese act (e.g. *Chung Ling Soo*) or else introduced a Chinese section into their full act (e.g. *Phillippe, Lyle*).

Chinese Sticks. A later development of the *Pillars of Solomon*. Here the two sticks are not joined at the bottom and can be separated, though at first the performer, as a *sucker* gag, pretends that they *are* joined, and separates them only after some by-play. Each stick is hollow and works independently of the other, the strings being actuated by a small weight which pulls the string up when the stick is held upright. Adroitness is needed to present the trick effectively.

Ching Ling Foo (Chee Ling Qua, *b* 1854). Perhaps the first Chinese magician to achieve personal fame

37

in the West. He was first apprenticed to a troupe of performers in Tientsin. His reputation became international when he visited New York in 1899. Here a sensation was caused by his colourful magic, which included the production of large bowls of water from a silk scarf, and a long coloured pole from his mouth. Visits to European theatres, including the Empire Theatre, London, made Chinese magic quite the fashion. His style of show directly inspired William Robinson to become the great *Chung Ling Soo*.

Chop Cup. Version of the *Cups and Balls* using only one cup and a *faked* ball; *illustration 40*.

40. Chop cup.

Chopper Effects. Type of illusion involving a small guillotine. The blade is first allowed to fall on a vegetable, slicing it cleanly in two. An assistant, sometimes a volunteer, is then induced to place his neck in the pillory. Again the blade falls, but without injuring the victim. Smaller versions involving the hand or finger are sometimes used; *illustration 41*. *Goodliffe* featured an effective-

looking leg chopper. See Baron, *MAGIC SIMPLIFIED*, pp.89–91; Goodliffe, *SIMPLY WIZARD*, pp.80–5.

chosen card. One selected and noted by a spectator.

Christopher, Milbourne. Prominent American magician, famous both as a performer and as one of the leading present-day writers on magic. He has toured the world with a big magic show, and is also author of a definitive biography of *Houdini*, two outstanding histories of magic, and two excellent books on so-called psychics: *SEERS, PSYCHICS AND ESP* (1970) and *MEDIUMS, MYSTICS & THE OCCULT* (1975). His remarkable collection of magic books and memorabilia has enabled him to supply some fascinating illustrations to his books. *History of magic*.

Chung Ling Soo (William E. Robinson, 1861–1918). American conjurer, at one time assistant to *Alexander Herrmann*. He failed to achieve more than moderate success under his own name and subsequently adopted oriental disguise. As Chung Ling Soo, the Marvellous Chinese Conjurer, he became one of the most notable performers in magical history, and his colourful act was immensely popular; *illustration 42*. While performing the *Bullet Catch* at the Wood Green Empire, London, he was mysteriously shot (23 March, 1918). The inquest resulted in a verdict of Death from Misadventure due to a defect in one of the guns. Rumours of suicide or murder, spread by some magical writers, seem to have no basis in fact. See Will Dexter, *THE RIDDLE OF CHUNG LING SOO* (1955). *Ching Ling Foo*.

cigarette manipulation. *Sleight-of-hand* with cigarettes, usually involv-

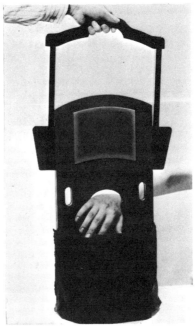

41. Hand or wrist chopper.

ing concealing cigarettes in the fingers, or *thumb-palming* them (*illustration 43*), or pinching them between the first and second fingers behind the hand, and then apparently producing them from the air. By apparently taking the cigarette in one hand but really retaining it (by thumb-palming) in the other, it can seemingly be passed right through the body or face. Lighted cigarettes are sometimes used, and can be produced from or vanished into the mouth by careful use of the tongue. See Hugard, MODERN MAGIC MANUAL, pp.211–34. *Card in Cigarette*; *Cardini*; *thumb tip*.

clairvoyance. Supposed ability to see incidents or persons remote in time or space, especially in conjunction with a *crystal ball*. *Second sight*; *mentalism*; *precognition*.

clean. With hands empty. The term 'left clean' is used particularly when a palmed article or a *gimmick* has been used in the course of a trick but is surreptitiously disposed of by the time the trick is concluded.

clip-board. Board of thin wood or thick cardboard with a sheet of paper attached to it by a bulldog clip at the top. The board is so faked that a carbon impression of any writing is left within it and can be removed behind the scenes, usually by an unseen assistant, who secretly conveys the information to the performer. It is sometimes used in

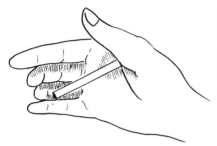

43. Cigarette thumb-palmed.

mentalism for the answering of questions written down by members of the audience.

Clock Dial. Clock face, usually glass or plastic, with a movable hand; *illustration 44*. An hour is chosen by a spectator and when the hand is spun round, it stops at the exact position on the dial. The secret is often a counter-weight which can be secretly adjusted on the pin in the centre of the hand in order to make it stop at any desired hour; *illustration 45*. Another method involves a hidden assistant and a length of strong thread which checks the movement of the hand. See Devant, THE BEST TRICKS, pp.66–74.

close-up magic. Tricks shown to spectators who are gathered round almost within touching distance of the performer. They are usually seated around a small table in one or more rows.

code. Method by which information is conveyed, usually by the performer, to a *medium* in *two-person telepathy*. There are two types of code: verbal

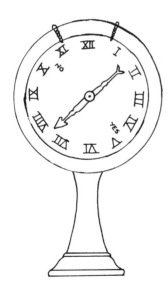

44. Clock dial.

45. Clock dial: adjustable counterweight in centre of removable clock hand.

41

and silent. In the former, medium and performer both learn a series of words each of which indicates something specific. Thus a sentence beginning with 'will' ('Will you tell us what this is?') might indicate a watch. Similarly, 'can' ('Can you say what this is?') might indicate a cigarette case. Such codes require a great deal of memorizing, and they sound artificial unless very well performed. Silent codes include action signals (e.g. left hand on lapel), positional signals (e.g. cards left at a particular place on table), and electric signals. Radio transmitting apparatus may sometimes be used. See Corinda, *13 STEPS TO MENTAL-ISM*, pp.237–70.

coil. Roll of paper or silk ribbon which can fit into a very small space but which, when unrolled, makes an impressive show. A small one can be slipped in the mouth; larger ones are used for production from box, hat, or *tambourine*. They are best uncoiled at speed with rhythmic movements of the performer's arm. *ribbon fountain*.

coin box. *Okito coin box*.

coin, folding. Coin cut into three pieces which are then invisibly joined with rubber. The coin can thus be secretly folded and inserted in a narrow opening (e.g. the neck of a bottle). The coin should be substituted for an unfaked one, which may be borrowed. The bottle trick has long been featured by a clever and amusing professional magician, *Billy McComb*.

coin holder. Device for retaining coins and releasing them one at a time as they are required, particularly useful in the *Aerial Treasury*.

coin in bottle. *coin, folding*.

coin shell. *shell*.

coin tray. Small tray for use in a trick where a few coins are to be secretly added to a collection already on the tray. A flat tube on the underside of the tray is filled with the extra coins, and all the coins are tipped out together into a hat or other container; *illustration 46*. Coins equivalent in number to those in the tube can now be vanished, and will appear to have travelled by magic to the hat. A similar device can be made with a dinner plate filled in at the bottom with stout white cardboard in which a narrow tunnel has

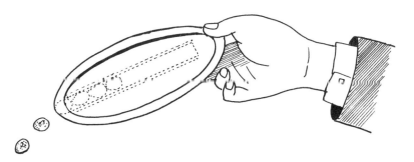

46. Coin tray.

47. Coin wand.

been cut. See Robinson, *MAGIC AS A PASTIME*, pp.69–70.

coin wand. Hollow wand in which is concealed a *folding coin*. By moving a small sliding knob in the wand the coin may be made to appear at the top of the wand; *illustration 47*. It can be used in connection with the *Aerial Treasury*, though it is not often seen nowadays.

colour-changing silk. Handkerchief that is made to change colour merely by passing the hand over it. Basically there are two handkerchiefs, different in colour, stitched together in such a way that they form a kind of bag, with a small ring in one corner. When the ring is drawn down, the bag is in effect turned inside out and the other colour is revealed. The silk is obtainable from magic dealers. *dye tube*.

Coloured Sands. Trick of Indian origin in which sands of three or four different colours are stirred up in a large bowl of water. A spectator is asked to name one of the colours. The performer plunges his hand into the bowl, grabs a handful of the mixture, and then lets fall a stream of dry sand of the chosen colour. The early secret was that little blocks of sand had previously been formed by mixing sand with melted wax or candle grease. Each colour had its own shape: thus blue might be a round block, red a square one, brown conical. The blocks were hidden in the loose sand tipped into the bowl. Nowadays thin rubber or polythene bags may replace the blocks, being slit with a fingernail at the appropriate moment.

cone. Apparatus for vanishing silks or other small articles, and made from newspaper or wrapping paper. Two sheets of identical size, roughly 40 cm (14 in) square, are pasted together (and trimmed) in such a way that a long triangular pocket is left extending from one corner towards the corner diagonally opposite, *illustration 48*. The paper is shown as a single sheet, rolled into a cone, and the silks are placed within (actually going into the pocket). When the paper is unwrapped the silks are seen to have vanished. Specially made cones which open out flat can be bought from some magic dealers; *illustration 50*. See Hoffmann, *LATER MAGIC*, pp.134–8; Tarbell, *COURSE, VOL. II*, pp.79–81. Note that the Tarbell cone is made in a slightly different way; *illustration 49*.

confederate

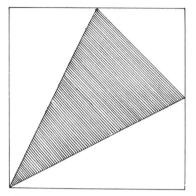

48. Paper prepared for making cone, showing triangular pocket (unpasted).

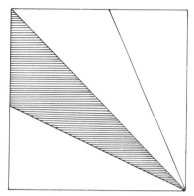

49. Tarbell cone, shaded area left unpasted.

50. Dealer's cone (Supreme Magic Co.).

confederate. Also stooge, plant, accomplice: person who secretly assists the conjurer while pretending to be an ordinary member of the audience. Though freely used in earlier times, confederacy has long been eschewed by most reputable conjurers, except for some occasional purpose. Unfortunately the use of a stooge for certain tricks is occasionally advocated in a few modern conjuring books. This is psychologically unsound, and such tricks are best disregarded. An amateur conjurer who cannot show an audience a few tricks without having to depend on the secret help of one of the friends he is supposed to be entertaining, not only brings his own performance into disrepute but also lowers the prestige of conjuring as an art, reducing it to a mere hoax. It is *essential*, especially in mental magic, that the audience should be convinced that no confederates are used, and it will be very hard to achieve this if one friend knows that you *are* using him as a stooge. The news will get around. A *volunteer* should never be secretly asked to act as an accomplice. He will not only have a pretty low opinion of your magical skill but is sure to pass on his opinion to others. An *assistant*, openly used, must of course be distinguished from a confederate.

conjurer. Person who, in former times, was supposed to conjure up spirits and demons. Before the late eighteenth century a sleight-of-hand performer was most often known as a juggler, and his art as juggling or legerdemain. The first use of 'conjurer' to denote a magical entertainer was probably in the book *THE CONJURER UNMASKED*, translated from the French in 1785. 'Conjuror' is a variant spelling, now generally obsolete.

'Conjurer Dick'. Well-known novel by *Angelo Lewis*, dealing realistically with the adventures of a lad who becomes assistant to a professional conjurer. Published by Frederick Warne (1886).

conjurer's choice. System whereby a card, word, number, etc. is *forced* upon a spectator although he is apparently given a free choice. If his choice suits the conjurer, the latter accepts it. If not, he pretends that the spectator has chosen the item to be discarded. The scheme often works without being detected, but it has a dangerous side. Normally a person who chooses something expects his choice to be used. It is better, therefore, to use the chosen item *in some way* rather than to discard it, and this may easily be done if the spectator is not first told the purpose of the choice.

contact mind-reading. *muscle-reading*.

continuity gag. Trick which the performer attempts unsuccessfully after each trick in his act, but finally accomplishes. See De Courcy, *GENIAL IMPROBABILITIES*, pp.55–62.

continuous back and front palm. Sleight by which the hand is shown 'empty' both sides by secretly transferring an article from the front to the back of the hand and vice versa in a smooth, continuous movement. To be really convincing it requires great skill and address. *back-palm*.

Cooke, George Alfred (1825–1905). Friend of *J. N. Maskelyne* and joint exposer of the *Davenport Brothers* in 1865. Subsequently the two men performed together as 'Maskelyne and Cooke' for 30 years. Though 10 years older than his friend, Cooke was never a formal partner at the *Egyptian Hall*, but received a salary.

costume act. One performed in period or foreign dress, often oriental.

court card. One of the picture playing-cards – King, Queen, or Jack.

Cremer, W. H., Junr. Mid-Victorian magic dealer with a shop in Regent Street, London. His name is given as the editor/translator of some very popular magic books of the early 1870s. They were mainly adapted,

crimp

51. Crystal ball, held by mentalist Stanton Carlisle.

probably by a hack writer, from French or American books. Their titles were: *THE SECRET OUT* (1871), *THE MAGICIAN'S OWN BOOK* (1871), *HANKY PANKY* (1872), *MAGIC NO MYSTERY* (1876).

crimp. To bend the corner of a card secretly so that it can be quickly found again. The word is also used by some conjurers as a synonym for *bridge*.

cut. To remove the upper half of a pack of cards. To complete the cut is to place the lower half on top of the former upper half, so that the two halves are reversed in position.

cut and restored string/rope. *string, cut and restored*.

cut, false. An apparent cutting of the pack which in fact leaves the cards in exactly the same order. With the pack in the left hand, make a *break* with the little finger. The right hand, covering the cards, takes the lower half of the pack as if it were the upper half and places it on the table. The rest of the cards (ostensibly the lower half) are now placed on top of those on the table. There are various other methods, but whatever form of false cut is used it should be done casually, while talking to the audience. See Clive, *CARD TRICKS*

46

52. The Cups and Balls performed by Prince Charles.

WITHOUT SKILL, pp.19–23. *under-cut*.

crystal ball. Used by some *mentalists* as an impressive piece of equipment in connection with *predictions* and *divinations*, the performer pretending to see the required card or name in the crystal; *illustration 51*. A spectator can actually see his own card if a miniature of a forced card is palmed and the crystal placed over it. Crystal gazing is technically known as scrying.

cull. To withdraw or arrange cards secretly while looking through or shuffling the pack.

Cups and Balls. Perhaps the oldest of all popular conjuring tricks, per-formed in East and West alike. Three goblets are placed upside down, and a small ball is made to appear and vanish beneath each cup and apparently to pass from cup to cup. The routine often continues with a larger ball or other object being unexpectedly found under one or more cups. The feats are achieved by elementary sleight-of-hand and subtle misdirection. *Illustration 52*. See Baron, *CLOSE-UP MAGIC FOR BEGINNERS*, pp.118–26; Elliott, *CLASSIC SECRETS OF MAGIC*, pp.176–206; Hugard, *MODERN MAGIC MANUAL*, pp.146–57.

Dancing Cane

53. Dante at the Garrick Theatre, London.

D

Dancing Cane. Popular trick in which the performer's cane moves about in various directions, even swinging around in circles, without apparently being touched. It is worked by the use of thread, and requires a good deal of practice to achieve the fluency of movement necessary for real effectiveness.

Dancing Handkerchief. Stage trick with a borrowed handkerchief, which is tied in one or more knots to resemble a sort of puppet. The performer makes mesmeric passes over it, causing it to leap off the table and perform a grotesque dance. A wand may be waved around it and a chair placed over it, indirectly proving that it is not fixed to a thread above it, but it continues to dance. The effect is achieved by a horizontal thread usually actuated by hidden assistants in the wings. It is a simple trick featured with great success by *Blackstone* and *Calvert*.

Dante (Harry Jansen, 1882–1955). Imposing Danish-born magician taken to America as a child. Up to 1923 he performed as The Great Jansen, but in that year he was hired to take one of *Thurston*'s road shows on tour under the name Dante. After covering America he went to Europe, opening with his own show which he called '*Sim Sala Bim*'. He was a masterly showman, very striking in appearance, with silver hair, a little goatee beard, and a commanding yet humorous manner. Among his specialities were a routine in which he posed as a lazy magician, allowing his assistants to do all the work, and an amusing illusion where he apparently allowed his audience to have a behind-the-scenes view of an assistant appearing from an empty box. *Illustration 53*. See also *Kalanag*.

Davenport Brothers (Ira 1839–1911, William 1841–77). Prominent spiritualist mediums whose effect on magical entertainment was considerable. Though apparently firmly tied inside a cabinet, they caused various musical instruments to be played, ostensibly by spirits. They were skilful performers, and could have achieved honest and well-deserved fame as escape artists. As they pretended to possess supernatural assistance, they were exposed time and again by leading conjurers, including *Anderson, Maskelyne, Herrmann*, and *Kellar* (who was at one time their assistant). *Davenport Cabinet*.

Davenport Cabinet. Piece of furniture rather like a wardrobe, in which the *Davenport Brothers* performed their feats; *illustration 54*. The name was also given to a small apparatus for obtaining secret possession of a coin, ring, or other article of similar size. A drawer fitted into a bottomless case, and pressure at a certain spot caused the hinged bottom of the drawer to drop down, allowing the article to fall into the performer's hand.

Davenport, Lewis (George Ryan, 1883–1916). Accomplished conjurer who performed a great many

54. The Davenport Brothers in their cabinet. (Robert-Houdin, 'Stage Conjuring'.)

times at *St George's Hall* and who invented many tricks, notably a colour-changing waistcoat and an ingenious version of the *Sunshade Trick*. At an early age he opened a magic shop in the East End of London, moving to the West End 12 years later. In due course control of the business passed to his son George (1906–62), and is now in the hands of his grand-daughter. The present shop is at 51 Great Russell Street, opposite the British Museum.

Dawes, Edwin A., Ph.D., D.Sc. Professor of Biochemistry at Hull University and well-known amateur magician, notable as a magical historian. Has for several years contributed regular and important histori-

cal articles to THE MAGIC CIRCULAR. A history of magic is due 1979.

deal, false. *false deal.*

dealers. A surprising number of people have made a living by making and/or selling magical apparatus; they have played an important part in the development of conjuring. Dealers constantly provide new tricks, and their shops have often been informal meeting-places for conjurers as well as markets for buying and selling. Quite a number of distinguished conjurers (e.g. *Hartz, LeRoy, Cardini, Murray, Harbin*) have at some time acted as magic dealers or as salesmen at the magic departments of large stores such as *Hamley*'s and *Gamage*'s. Among the leading

55. Dealer's stand at a magic convention.

dealers today may be mentioned *Supreme Magic Co.* (Bideford), *Davenport* (London), *International Magic Studio* (London), Hughes (Norfolk), and in the U.S.A., Tannen (New York), Abbott (Michigan), Magic Inc. (Chicago), and Kanter (Philadelphia). There are numerous others, and up-to-date names and addresses of dealers will be found in the advertisement pages of such magical journals as *ABRACADABRA*, *GENII*, and *THE LINKING RING*. *Illustration 55*.

De Biere, Arnold (1878–1934). One of the greatest magicians of this century, billed as 'The Man of Mystery', which he was – not only on the stage but in his private life, details of which are scanty. Possibly of continental origin, he was partly American, but lived in England for much of his later life. The outstanding characteristic of his performances was artistry, both in large illusions such as Bride of the Air (*Asrah*) and in manipulations, which were always a great feature of his well-balanced act. Though not a great inventor, he was able to give a personal quality to familiar tricks, and his *Egg Bag* and *Thumb Tie* were justly famous.

Decapitation Trick. The first recorded conjuring trick was *Dedi*'s feat of cutting off the head of a fowl and then restoring it. In due course it became fashionable to treat a human being in a similar way, and one of the tricks revealed in Scot's *DISCOVERIE OF WITCHCRAFT* was 'to cut off one's head, and to laie it in a platter, &c: which the jugglers call the decollation of John Baptist'. 'John Baptist' lay on a table with his head sunk into a hole. The head of a man beneath the table was pushed up through another hole, revealing a head without a visible body; *illustration 56*. Brimstone was put in a brazier 'to make the sight more dreadfull'. A large cloth often concealed the front of the table. *Maskelyne* adapted the feat to present a sketch in which a quack doctor 'cured' a country bumpkin of a buzzing in the head by cutting it off, only to find that the severed head continued to express its feelings. A similar effect was performed by many other magicians. See also *chopper effects*.

deck. American term for a pack of cards, used also in sixteenth-century England.

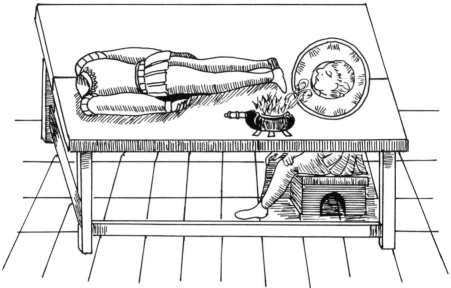

56. Decapitation in Elizabethan England.

De Courcy, Ken. Experienced magician and ideas man, editor of *MAGIGRAM* and author of several useful booklets, the most substantial of which is *GENIAL IMPROBABILITIES* (1949, 1968).

Dedi. First conjurer whose name has been recorded. According to the *Westcar Papyrus* the magician performed conjuring tricks for King Cheops, builder of the Great Pyramid, nearly 5,000 years ago. His main feat was apparently cutting off and replacing the heads of a goose and a pelican – a trick which fairground performers and even well known magicians such as *Bosco* were still showing thousands of years later. *Decapitation Trick*.

De Kolta (Joseph Buatier, 1847–1903). French-born magical inventor and performer, most of whose appearances were in England and America. Though not outstanding as a performer and showman, he possessed the most inventive mind in nineteenth-century magic. Among his many original illusions were the *Birdcage Vanish*, the *Vanishing Lady*, the production of *spring flowers* from a cone, and the Expanding Die, a clever trick in which a small die expanded until it was large enough to hold a young woman. De Kolta was his mother's maiden name, which he adopted professionally. He died in America, but his body was brought to England for burial.

Demon Handkerchief. *Handkerchief, Demon.*

Devant, David (David Wighton, 1868–1941). By general consent the greatest magician of his time, by reason of his inventiveness, his attention to detail, and above all the easy charm of his stage personality. In 1913 he received the unique tribute of a special presentation from fellow magicians in recognition of

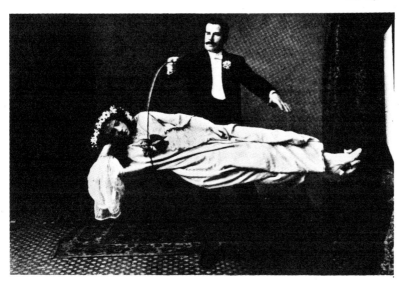

57. Devant and the Floating Lady.

the services he had rendered to the art of magic. He first came into prominence in 1893, when he joined *Maskelyne* at the *Egyptian Hall*. On the removal to *St George's Hall* in 1905 he became a partner, and 'Maskelyne and Devant' became even more famous than 'Maskelyne and Cooke' had been. In 1915 the partnership was dissolved and Devant devoted his attention to the big variety theatres of Britain. But within a few years he was stricken with incurable illness and entered a nursing home at Putney, where he remained for the rest of his life. His little books *MAGIC MADE EASY* (1903) and *TRICKS FOR EVERYONE* (1910), together with his section of *OUR MAGIC*, were classics of their kind. After his illness he was able by dictation to continue his writings, which include *LESSONS IN CONJURING* (1922), *MY MAGIC LIFE* (1931), and *SECRETS OF MY MAGIC* (1935). *Illustration 57. Artist's Dream.*

Devil of a Hat. *Hartz*; *hat productions*.

Dexter, William (William T. Pritchard). Journalist by profession, now retired, and a lively and accomplished writer of magical books. A specialist in mentalism, author of *FEATURE MAGIC FOR MENTALISTS* (1975); a magical historian, his book on *Chung Ling Soo* being an important contribution to magical literature (1955); author of useful books for beginners, such as *101 MAGIC SECRETS* (1957) in comic-strip form, and *EVERYBODY'S BOOK OF MAGIC* (1956).

diachylon. Lead plaster, an adhesive substance used for rubbing on a card to make it adhere temporarily to the next, a use believed to have been discovered by Hofzinser. See Hugard, *ENCYCLOPEDIA OF CARD TRICKS*, pp.126–30. *rough-and-smooth*.

Dickens, Charles (1812–70). Dickens was an enthusiastic amateur conjurer and a keen spectator. John Forster's *LIFE OF CHARLES DICKENS* (1871–4) contains a long account of a performance given at Boulogne about 1854 by a skilful French conjurer who has been identified as the Chevalier de Caston. There are many references to magic in *HOUSEHOLD WORDS* and *ALL THE YEAR ROUND*, including a long article in the latter on the history of conjuring (April 19, 1862). See Findlay, *CHARLES DICKENS AND HIS MAGIC* (1962).

die. Singular form of 'dice', which is a plural word and should not be used for a single die. Although small dice are sometimes used in *close-up magic*, a conjuring die is usually 10 or 12 cm (about 4 in) square.

die box, sliding. Apparatus often used as a *sucker trick*. An oblong box with two side-by-side compartments is shown empty and a large die is placed in one side of it; *illustration 58*. There are two doors at the front and two at the back, and when these are closed the performer pretends to vanish the die. He shows first one side of the box empty, then the other. But as he tilts the box each time, producing a sliding sound, the spectators are convinced that the die simply slides from side to side. Ultimately, with sham reluctance, he opens all four doors at once, revealing that the box really is empty. The vanished die is a *shell*, open on two sides, though a hinged flap allows it to appear solid; an unfaked die is now produced from a borrowed hat. See Devant, *THE BEST TRICKS*, pp.75–80; Page, *THE BIG BOOK OF MAGIC*, pp.235–7.

Diminishing Cards. Trick in which some ordinary playing-cards appear to be squeezed smaller and smaller, finally vanishing altogether. Palming and substitution usually account for the mystery. Lang Neil, *THE MODERN CONJURER*, pp.92–6; Devant, *LESSONS IN CONJURING*, pp.20–6; Hugard and Braue, *ROYAL ROAD TO CARD MAGIC*, pp.287–9.

discover. *card discovery*.

'Discoverie of Witchcraft, The'. First book in English to explain genuine conjuring tricks in detail, which it does in one section. However, the real purpose of the author, Reginald Scot, was to prove that apparent miracle-workers were not really in league with the devil, and hence should not be persecuted. Such an anti-persecution attitude offended

58. Sliding die box.

the credulous James I, a great believer in the power of witchcraft, and he ordered the book to be publicly destroyed. First printed in 1584, it has been reprinted more than once, a recent reprint (1974) unfortunately containing an unsatisfactory introduction by Montague Summers from the 1930 edition.

distraction. Drawing the attention of the audience away from a secret move by creating a diversion (e.g. dropping something or making a strong gesticulation with the other hand). This should not be confused with true *misdirection*, which is a more subtle art, permeating a whole routine. Distraction can be used successfully only on isolated occasions.

ditch. Secretly discard an article no longer needed.

divided pack. Cards *set-up* with all of one kind (e.g. black) at the top, and all of the other kind (e.g. red) at the bottom. *Odds and Evens.*

divination. In occultism the term denotes prophecy (*prediction*), but to conjurers it means finding the identity of a chosen card, word, or number by some form of *mentalism*. However easy the process may really be, the performer should suggest some mental effort and uncertainty.

Dizzy Limit, The. Illusion first presented by *Oswald Williams*. A girl climbs into a net hammock, which is then hoisted into mid air. A pistol is fired, and with a scream the girl suddenly vanishes. *Jasper Maskelyne* afterwards featured the trick.

Do As I Do. A classic card trick. A spectator takes a pack of playing-cards and is asked to follow the movements made by the performer with another pack. An interchange of packs often follows. Finally, after

the spectator and the performer have each chosen a card independently, it turns out that they have selected precisely the same one. There are several variations and methods. Scarne, *SCARNE ON CARD TRICKS*, pp.27–30; Hugard, *ENCYCLOPEDIA OF CARD TRICKS*, pp.74–90; Clive, *CARD TRICKS WITHOUT SKILL*, pp.60–1; Hugard and Braue, *ROYAL ROAD TO CARD MAGIC*, pp.83–4.

Döbler, Ludwig Leopold (1801–64). Viennese conjurer noted for his charm and skill. After scoring many successes he came to England in 1842, billed as Louis Döbler, and was equally popular. He retired in 1848 at the height of his fame and was honoured in his own city of Vienna by having a street named after him.

Doll's House. Illusion originally presented by Fred Culpitt at *St George's Hall*. A large doll's house is shown empty and a small doll placed within. Suddenly a real live doll, twice the size of the house appears in place of the toy. Concealment is usually within the table-top (deceptive in depth) and the back of the house.

double-backed card. One which shows a back on both sides, having no *face*. An ordinary pack with backs to match is usually required to go with the double-backed card. Obtainable from dealers.

double-faced card. One with a *face* on both sides. The face should be similar in style to the faces of the performer's ordinary pack. Obtainable from dealers.

double lift. Useful sleight which involves showing the two top cards as if they were only one; the spectators are misled into thinking that the second card from the top is the top card. There are several ways of accomplishing the lift, but it is usual for the cards to be held at each end between finger and thumb. The *move* needs to be made smoothly and without the least hesitation. See Baron, CARD TRICKS FOR BEGINNERS, pp.34–5; Gibson, COMPLETE ILLUSTRATED BOOK OF CARD TRICKS, pp.154–7; Hugard, ENCYCLOPEDIA OF CARD TRICKS, pp.422–3.

dove magic. A form of conjuring in which doves are produced and/or vanished. It was popularized after the last war by a suave American, Channing Pollock. Many imitators followed his lead, and doves tended to appear in conjuring shows ad nauseam. Before production the birds are usually confined in a holder, a sort of bag with holes for head and tail, and often hidden within the performer's clothing. They are produced by inserting a thumb or finger in a loop attached to the bag. Some spectators greet the appearance of a dove with approval; others find this use of livestock disagreeable. The beginner is strongly advised to avoid it and to confine himself to the many kinds of magic which offend no one. *animals in magic*.

dove pan. Old-fashioned apparatus for apparently producing doves or other livestock from flames. Paper is put in a shallow round pan and set alight. The flames are extinguished with a faked lid in which two or three doves are closely confined. The container is left behind when the lid proper is removed, and the unfortunate birds make their appearance. This kind of apparatus is best used (if at all) for the production of sweets, etc.

dovetail shuffle. Mixing the cards by dividing them into two halves, placing these corner to corner, and gradually releasing the corners so that the cards become interlaced. Also known as riffle shuffle. See Hugard and Braue, ROYAL ROAD TO CARD MAGIC, pp.42–6.

Downs, Thomas Nelson (1867–1938). American conjurer who specialized in coin manipulation; known as 'The King of Koins'. He started his career as a railway clerk but practised coin sleights assiduously and scored immediate success when he turned professional conjurer. Although his was mainly a coin act, his skill brought him fame even on the stages of big variety theatres. He became one of the most highly paid magicians of his day. The book THE ART OF MAGIC (1909), published under his name, was largely written by J. N. Hilliard. *Aerial Treasury*.

drawer-box. Apparatus for producing and vanishing small articles. The drawer is really a double one. When the outer drawer only is pulled out it appears empty; the inner drawer, containing a handkerchief, etc., is left hidden in the box. A twist of the drawer handle enables the inner drawer to be brought out and the handkerchief revealed. Reversing the process results in the disappearance of an article.

drawing-room magic. Conjuring on a fairly small scale, using not very elaborate apparatus, and often performed before friends in a private house. In early Victorian times it was often called 'parlour magic'. It has some affinities with modern *close-up magic*, but there was often a perceptible gap between performer and audience.

drumhead tube. Metal tube about 13 cm (5 in) long, with a flat ring fitting over each end; *illustration 60*. The tube is shown empty, and pieces of

59. Drumhead tube: conical gimmick.

60. Drumhead tube and rings.

61. Handkerchief produced from drumhead tube.

thin paper are placed over the ends and kept in place with the two rings. In due course the paper at one end is pierced, and a previously vanished handkerchief is found therein; *illustration 61*. The secret lies in a conical gimmick (*illustration 59*) sharply pointed at one end and the same size as the drumhead at the other end. This is covered with similar thin paper and contains a duplicate of the handkerchief that was vanished. The performer palms the gimmick and at the right moment secretly pushes it into one end of the tube.

Dunninger, Joseph (1892–1975). American *mentalist*, born in Manhattan of German immigrant parents. In his youth he performed a straightforward magic routine, but later he added escapes, *Blindfold Drives*, and mind-reading; by 1919 he was almost exclusively a mentalist, showing a strong sense of showmanship. American TV advanced his fame after World War II. By this time he was affecting genuine telepathic power, as his book, *WHAT'S ON YOUR MIND?*, rather portentously exemplified, and his claims drew strong criticism from some fellow magicians. The appearance in the 1960s of a young rival, *Kreskin*, aroused Dunninger's own indignation. His *COMPLETE ENCYCLOPEDIA OF MAGIC* (1967, 1970) is misnamed; it is in fact a bulky mixture of parlour tricks and stage illusion exposures, largely in comic strip form.

dye tube. Gimmick for apparently dyeing white handkerchiefs, which are pushed into a rolled-up paper cylinder and emerge at the other end a different colour. The gimmick, a small metal or cardboard tube containing the coloured handkerchiefs, is secretly introduced into the cylinder as this is being formed. The white handkerchiefs enter the tube, displacing the coloured ones, and the tube is then allowed to drop secretly into (say) a chair *servante*, after which the paper cylinder can be casually unrolled. See Hay, *AMATEUR MAGICIAN'S HANDBOOK*, pp.251–2; Devant, *LESSONS IN CONJURING*, pp.62–71.

57

E

effect. Description of a trick as seen by the audience. The word is sometimes used also as an alternative to *trick*.

egg bag. Small cloth bag from 20 to 30 cm (8 to 12 in) long and a little less in width. There is a long, secret pocket inside the bag, usually with its opening downward when the bag is held normal way up. If an egg is put in the bag and the latter held upside down the egg will be retained in the pocket instead of falling from the bag. A true master of magic can make this simple fact the basis of an immensely entertaining routine lasting for 10 minutes. *De Biere* was noted for his brilliant handling of this effect. See Hugard, *MODERN MAGIC MANUAL*, pp.166–8 (with a slightly different pocket arrangement); Elliott, *CLASSIC SECRETS OF MAGIC*, pp.96–106; Robinson, *MAGIC AS A PASTIME*, pp.77–9.

egg, hollow. Also *Stodare egg*. Artificial egg with a hole in one side, thus allowing a *silk* to be changed into an egg. It is now fairly well known, and has even been used as a *sucker gag* by some conjurers, who reveal the secret.

Eggs, Boy, and Girl. Amusing trick originated and made famous by *Devant*, using two young volunteers. The performer covered his hand with a bowler hat, previously shown empty, and suddenly discovered an egg in his fingers. He handed it to a small girl, who in turn passed it to a small boy. The same action was repeated again and again, until the boy's arms were so full of eggs that these began to fall. In pre-1914 days, when eggs were cheap and plentiful, the trick proved hilarious.

Egyptian Hall. Former building in Piccadilly, London, erected in 1812 as a museum. Later it was used for various exhibitions and shows, including magical performances by *Robin*, *Stodare*, and *Herrmann*. In 1873 *Maskelyne and Cooke* booked a room at the Hall for three weeks. They stayed for 30 years, and the name of the Hall became synonymous with *Maskelyne* and the Home of Mystery. The building was demolished in 1905. *Illustration 62*. See Lamb, *VICTORIAN MAGIC*; Jenness, *MASKELYNE & COOKE*.

Eight Kings set-up. One of the oldest systems for a *prearranged* pack of cards. It is based on the nonsense couplet:

Eight kings threatened to save
Ninety-five ladies for one sick knave.

This makes it easy to remember the order:

8 K 3 10 2 7
9 5 Q 4 A 6 J

Suits are arranged in any regular order, such as C H S D (CHaSeD). The earliest reference to the system is probably to be found in *THE MAGICIAN'S OWN BOOK* (New York, 1859); *Cremer*. Because the Eight Kings set-up has been disclosed in so many books over the years, and may thus be known to some spectators, variations of it are

62. Interior of the Egyptian Hall.

sometimes used. Here is a new one:

Eighteen kings once fought to save Thirty-nine queens (from) five sick knaves.

8	10	K	A	4	2	7
3	9	Q	5	6	J	

See Reed, *MAGICAL MIRACLES YOU CAN DO*, pp.24–6; Hoffmann, *MODERN MAGIC*, pp.50–1; Devant, *MAGIC MADE EASY*, pp.94–6.

electric pack. Special pack of cards; these are connected with short pieces of thin white string, enabling certain card flourishes to be performed without much skill. Sometimes used (and exposed) by comedy magicians.

Elmsley Count. False count whereby four cards are counted as four but one is counted twice and one not counted at all.

entertainment. The main purpose of any conjuring performance. If the spectators are not entertained by a trick, no matter how clever it is, then the trick is a failure. Even a simple trick can be very entertaining if it is presented with point and pungency.

Erdnase, S. W. Pen-name of a writer, believed to be a reformed gambler, whose book *THE EXPERT AT THE CARD TABLE* (1902) exposed card gamblers' methods and formed the basis of many card sleights used in conjuring. The author's real name was probably Milton Andrews, for many years believed to be E. S. Andrews.

escapology. Branch of magical entertainment in which the performer is secured in some apparently adequate manner but succeeds in escaping. Escapes may be made from

59

63. Alan Alan escaping from a strait-jacket while suspended on a burning rope.

handcuffs, ropes, chains, sacks, boxes, mailbags, strait-jackets, and various other kinds of restraint. They may be carried out in a room, on a stage, suspended from a high building or a crane many feet above the ground (*illustration 63*), or plunged beneath the surface of a river. The first man to bring this type of feat into prominence was *Houdini*. In addition to performing the above-named escaping feats he devised many ingenious variations, including escapes from milk churns and from a cabinet filled with water into which he was placed upside down; *illustration 148*. He also made a feature of escaping from prison cells. Among present-day specialists in this line are *Howard Peters* and *Alan Alan. Hardeen*; *Murray*; *Box Trick*; *sack escapes*; *Water Torture Cell*.

ESP. Abbreviation for 'extra-sensory perception', the ability (real or supposed) to perceive without the employment of any of the normal five senses; it embraces telepathy, clairvoyance, and precognition. Despite multitudinous experiments by Dr Rhine and others, which have satisfied some people, the validity of ESP remains controversial. However, some mentalists lay claim to it in order to encourage spectators to take a real interest in their 'telepathic' feats. This is legitimate for entertainment purposes, but if the pretence is overdone it becomes indistinguishable from charlatanry. Trickery should not seriously masquerade as scientific truth.

ESP cards. Used for serious experiments in ESP, these are usually produced in packs of 25. Five symbols are each repeated five times: star, circle, square, cross, and waves (three parallel wavy lines); *illustration 64*. Magicians sometimes use these cards for certain *mentalism* feats, partly for effect, partly as a change from ordinary playing-cards. See Trost, *ESP SESSION WITH NICK TROST*; Kolb, *EXCITING EXPERIMENTS IN ESP*, pp.14–19.

Evans, Henry Ridgely (1861–1949). Well-known American magical historian, whose *THE OLD AND THE NEW MAGIC* (1906) is one of the classics of conjuring literature. Though legally qualified, he spent his working life as a journalist and as editor in the Office of Education. Among his other books are: *HOURS WITH THE GHOSTS* (1897), *MAGIC AND ITS PROFESSORS* (1902), and *HISTORY OF CONJURING AND MAGIC* (1928).

Evaporated Milk. Popular and effective trick with a fake perspex milk jug which appears to be full of milk.

The contents are seemingly poured into a paper cone until almost all the milk is gone. The performer then suddenly screws up the cone and tosses it towards the audience. The milk has gone. The jug has a false wall inside the exterior, and a small quantity of fake milk is poured into the space between the two and suggests a filled jug. This is easily 'emptied', the milk really entering the central compartment and showing as a small quantity at the bottom.

Everywhere and Nowhere. Famous card trick devised by *Hofzinser*, though there are now several versions. The performer puts three indifferent cards on the table. Then each in turn seems to become the same card, one previously chosen by a spectator. Finally they are shown to be indifferent cards once more. Sleight-of-hand, particularly the bottom change, is the secret. See Downs, THE ART OF MAGIC, pp.44–58; Hilliard, GREATER MAGIC, pp.567–70; Hugard and Braue, ROYAL ROAD TO CARD MAGIC, pp.271–4.

examination. Passing apparatus to spectators to prove it is free from trickery should not be overdone, for the constant handing out of articles to be looked at can interrupt the flow of a performance. Most people would rather be entertained than challenged to look for false bottoms, etc. that are obviously not there. If a spectator can be given a natural opportunity to handle apparatus during the course of a trick, that is better than an explicit invitation to look for *fakes*.

experiment. Term sometimes used by conjurers in place of *trick*. Suitable mainly for scientific, pseudo-scientific, or psychological tricks, and for *mentalism*.

'Expert at the Card Table, The'. *Erdnase*.

exposure. Disclosure of conjuring secrets – a practice to be avoided. If you give away the secret of a trick you cannot perform the same trick to the same people again. Moreover, indiscriminate exposure lowers the art of magic in public esteem; people are apt to be annoyed both with themselves and with the performer when they realize by what simple means they have been deceived. So NEVER tell how your tricks are done.

extra-sensory perception. *ESP*.

64. ESP cards.

F

face. The side of a playing-card with pips or picture showing. Thus a face-up card is one with the face uppermost, and a face-down card one with the face hidden and the back showing.

fake. A piece of apparatus seen by the audience but not exactly what it appears to be: e.g. the bottle in the *Bottle and Glass Trick*, the *shell* in the billiard ball multiplication, the *cone* for vanishing silks. *gimmick*.

fake cards. Cards specially made to enable particular tricks to be performed. They include cards with certain pips missing; with fanciful values (e.g. $3\frac{1}{2}$ clubs); with three or four values printed on a single card; *illustration 65. Double backs*; *double faces*; *nudist cards*; *flap card*.

faked. Term applied to an article that looks ordinary but has been secretly doctored in some way.

fakir. Indian wandering magician or mendicant.

false bottom. Extra bottom of a box or other container, situated a little above the base, and allowing space for various articles to be hidden between the true and false bottoms for subsequent production after the box has been shown apparently empty. Another type of false bottom presses (until released) against the back of the box or casket, with *spring flowers* or balls crushed behind it. A third type is found in the *Inexhaustible Box*. The term 'false-bottom school' was used critically a hundred years ago by *Robert-Houdin* to describe conjurers who

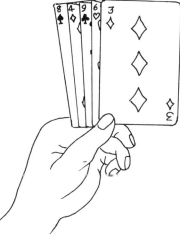

65. Fake card made to represent four cards fanned.

THE MAGIC CIRCLE

in association with

THE MAGIC COLLECTORS' ASSOCIATION

THE SECOND COLLECTORS' DAY

14th May, 1977

Headquarters of The Magic Circle in Chenies Mews

66. Magic Circle Collector's Day programme showing Isaac Fawkes.

63

depend entirely upon self-working apparatus.

false count. To count cards or coins in such a way as to make them seem either more numerous or less numerous than they really are. Used particularly in certain card tricks (e.g. *Six-card Repeat, Cards Across*). *buckle count; Elmsley count*. See Hugard, *MODERN MAGIC MANUAL*, pp.348–9; Hay, *AMATEUR MAGICIAN'S HANDBOOK*, p.95; Blackstone, *MODERN CARD TRICKS*, p.31.

false cut. *cut, false*.

false deal. Way of dealing cards so that some card other than the normal top card is dealt. The card dealt is usually either the second card from the top or the bottom card. *Second deal; bottom deal*.

false finger. *finger, false*.

false shuffle. Any type of *shuffle* which does not genuinely mix the cards but leaves some or all of them in a *prearranged* order. There are many varieties. See Gibson, *COMPLETE ILLUSTRATED BOOK OF CARD MAGIC*, pp.48–54; Clive, *CARD TRICKS WITHOUT SKILL*, pp.23–9.

fan. *card fan; breakaway*.

faro shuffle. If the ends of two sections of a pack are pressed together, the cards will first curl downward and then interlace themselves as they spring upward. This is known as a faro shuffle from the old gambling game of Faro.

Fawkes, Isaac (*d* 1731). Perhaps the most famous conjurer of his day. Though known mainly as a fairground performer he was no vagabond, and was said to have amassed quite a fortune. He appeared regularly at Bartholomew Fair and is pictured in Hogarth's *SOUTHWARK FAIR*. *Illustration 66*.

feint. An action which appears to be made but in fact is only simulated, as

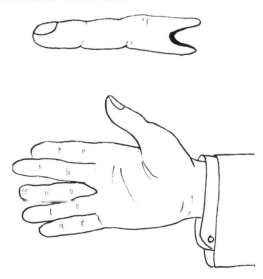

67. False finger.

when the performer feigns to take an article in his right hand but really leaves it in his left (e.g. by the *French drop*).

Findlay, James B. (1904–73). One of the most notable collectors of conjuring books and memorabilia. Born in Glasgow, in later years he settled in the Isle of Wight, where his home (for a while a private hotel) became a magical shrine visited by almost every conjurer of note. Catalogues of his fine collection of magical posters and of his library[1] were published in 1972 and 1975 respectively. He also published a number of useful books and booklets on aspects of conjuring history and collecting, mostly written by himself.

Find the Lady. *Three-card Trick.* Also a clever stage illusion, invented by Amac, in which three giant playing-cards are suspended above three stools, and a girl switches bewilderingly from stool to stool. See Hilliard, *GREATER MAGIC*, pp.965–8, though his method is dubious.

finger, false. Flesh-coloured plastic or metal finger with its open end shaped to fit into the fork of the middle fingers; *illustration 67*. When the hands are even slightly in motion the extra finger is very hard to detect. It is often used for the production or vanishing of a handkerchief. *drumhead tube*; *handkerchief vanish.*

finger-flinger. Sleight-of-hand performer. Generally used in a critical sense to indicate a conjurer more concerned with digital skill than with entertainment.

finger palm. Concealment of a ball, coin, etc. in the fingers, which should be held in a natural way, slightly curved.

fire-eating. Ancient art practised as

[1] Auctioned at Sotheby's in 1979.

an entertainment since the days of the Roman theatre. The most notable fire-eaters, perhaps, have been Richardson (seventeenth century), Powell (eighteenth century), and the Frenchman Xavier Chabert, known as the Fire King (early nineteenth century), who ate phosphorus, boiling oil, and molten lead, and sat in an oven while a leg of lamb was roasted. Modern fire-eaters mainly take mouthfuls of spirit and blow flames from their mouths, which is spectacular but tends to become monotonous. One of the best known today is Stromboli, who presents a striking though rather repetitious act. A brilliant picture of the life of a fire-eater and sword-swallower is given in Dan Mannix, *MEMOIRS OF A SWORD-SWALLOWER* (1951). See also L. H. Miller, *THRILLING MAGIC*, pp.7–21.

first conjuring trick. *decapitation*; *Dedi*; *Cups and Balls.*

fish-catching. Trick introduced by *Chung Ling Soo*. A fishing-line with hook baited is tossed towards the audience, when suddenly a goldfish is seen on the hook. The performer removes it and places it in a bowl, where it is seen swimming about. The bait conceals a dummy fish, released by a sudden jerk. This is *switched* for a live goldfish concealed in the rod handle in wet cottonwool. Several fish are usually produced in this way. Not every spectator cares for this kind of trick.

flap. *card box*; *slate flap.*

flap card. Fake card for *card changing*. A flap which is a *double-faced* half card is attached to the centre of the main card by a thin rubber spring. When the flap is held down it completes the value of the upper half of the main card. When it is allowed to spring up it completes the

68. Flap card.

value of the lower half. A wave of the card in the air covers the change. *Illustration 68.*

flash paper. Tissue paper chemically treated so that it disappears in a flash when ignited. Obtainable from magic dealers.

floating ball. Stage illusion in which a large but light ball rises in the air and floats about the stage. A hoop is often passed over it to indicate (seemingly) that there are no threads attached. Sometimes the thread is held by one or more assistants, sometimes by the performer himself. The trick is beautiful to watch when well handled. Other objects beside a ball have been made to float, perhaps the most effective being Rink's Flying Saucer and Nielsen's Floating Violin. *levitation; Okito; Zombie.* See Sorcar, *MAGIC*, pp.272–9; Walker, *SECRETS OF MODERN CONJURING*,

pp.140–3; Bamberg and Parrish, *OKITO ON MAGIC*, pp.47–51.

Floating Lady. *levitation; illustration 57.*

flourish. Display of skill not involving deception, usually with playing-cards: e.g. *fanning; springing.*

flower production. *bouquet, magic.*

Flying Sorcerers. Fellowship of magicians who have been invited to fly the Atlantic in either direction to entertain with magic. It was started in 1950 after *Goodliffe* had taken a party to America. Membership is by invitation only from the original founders; at present there are between 30 and 40 members. There is no subscription and there are no official meetings and no officers, but members have their own badge and tie.

Fogel, Maurice. Famous British *mentalist* who presents an impressive 'One Man Mystery Show', and who

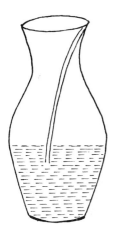

69. Foo can.

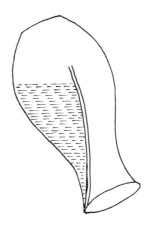

70. Inverted Foo can with water retained.

specializes in his own version of the *Bullet Catch* (*Russian Roulette*). He came to the fore as an entertainer during his army days in World War II. He has taken his mental act almost all over the world, and performed under all conditions, from private dinners to music halls and theatres.

folding coin. *coin, folding.*

Foo can. Vessel, originally used by *Ching Ling Foo*, for producing or vanishing water. One side of the can has a secret compartment, closed at the top, and extending downward for just over half the depth of the can; *illustration 69.* Water can be poured out normally if the can is held with the secret compartment on the upper side, but if it is held the other way up no water will come out; *illustration 70.*

force. Secretly compel a spectator to select something that meets the con-

jurer's wishes. There are many methods. *card force*; *changing bag*; *conjurer's choice*; *forcing pack*; *switch-box.*

forcing pack. Playing-cards which are all alike; hence when a spectator chooses one from a face-down fan or spread it is bound to be the one the performer wishes. A two-way forcing pack is one that has two different cards repeated many times. *card force.*

foulard. Scarf made of thin silk. *blind-fold.*

Four-Ace Trick. Classic card trick in which the four aces are put separately face down on the table and each has three indifferent cards placed on it. In due course the cards are turned face up, when it is seen that the four aces have come together. There are many versions, one of the oldest and best being Charles Bertram's, described in

French drop

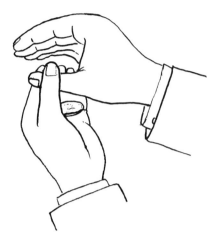

71. French drop: coin held in left hand.

72. French drop: coin drops past right thumb.

Hay, *AMATEUR MAGICIAN'S HAND-BOOK*, 49–51. See also Gibson, *WHAT'S NEW IN MAGIC*, pp.96–107; Adair, *CONJURING AS A CRAFT*, pp.63–70. An easy four-ace trick is in Reed, *MAGICAL MIRACLES YOU CAN DO*, p.24.

French drop. Sleight in which a small article appears to be taken in (say) the right hand from the left hand but in fact remains in the latter. A coin, for example, is held between the left finger and thumb, palm upward; *illustration 71*. The right hand, palm downward, seems to grasp it, but the coin drops past the right thumb and remains in the left hand; *illustration 72*. The performer should look at the right hand. *feint*; *misdirection*; *pass* (2); *simulation*.

Frikell, Wiljalba (1818–1903). Finnish or German magician usually credited with originating the wearing of ordinary evening dress for perform-

ing, and with being the first to abandon the use of elaborate apparatus and to depend on skill alone. Although these claims have been questioned, Frikell was certainly one of the first performers to simplify magical settings and equipment. He came to England in 1857 as 'a wizard without apparatus'.

Frost, Thomas (*b* 1821). Was author of the first history of magic as an entertainment, *LIVES OF THE CONJURERS* (1876). Frost was primarily a political journalist with no special interest in magic. But his *LIVES*, despite certain inaccuracies, is one of the great magical classics, and remained for 50 years the only significant history of the art of conjuring. *history of magic*.

Fu Manchu (David Bamberg, 1904–74). Son of *Okito*, and prominent illusionist who toured South

68

America with an impressive Chinese act, full of colour and drama. His father called it 'the climax of all the Bamberg shows'. He retired in 1966 to conduct a magic store in Buenos Aires.

funnel. Apparatus usually employed for comic effect. The funnel is made double, with enough space to contain a fair amount of liquid; *illustration 73*. If an airhole under the handle is closed with wax the funnel can be held mouth towards the audience to show it apparently empty. But if the mouth is placed, for instance, against a volunteer's forehead or elbow and the wax is removed from the airhole, a stream of liquid will pour from the spout. A common practice is to work the volunteer's other arm as though it were a pump-handle.

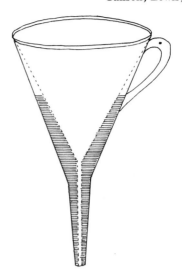

73. Magic funnel, with liquid in secret compartment.

G

gag. Joke.

Gamage's. Large department store in Holborn, London, founded by A. W. Gamage in 1878, which had a notable conjuring department, particularly in the first three or four decades of this century. Among the well-known magicians who served there were *Goldston*, for some years its manager, *Cardini*, *Harbin*, and Harry Baron. Gamage's conjuring catalogues, entitled *GAMAGIC*, are now collector's items. *dealers.*

Ganson, Lewis. One of the most prolific and important present-day writers on magic, specializing in sleight-of-hand. An expert photographer with a wide knowledge of magic and magicians, he has exercised a great influence on manipulative magic with his many excellent books, carefully illustrated. Among these are *THE DAI VERNON BOOK OF MAGIC* (1957),

69

THE ART OF CLOSE-UP MAGIC (1966), and MAGIC WITH FAUCETT ROSS (1975). Illustrations 27, 147.

Gaultier, Camille (1872–1943). French lawyer, author of LA PRESTIDIGITATION SANS APPAREIL (1914), one of the great classics on sleight-of-hand. Translated into English by Jean Hugard (1945), edited by Paul Fleming.

Geller, Uri. Israeli whose alleged supernormal powers, assisted by creatures from outer space, allowed him to bend spoons and keys, stop watches and clocks, and perform mentalism feats. The excitement aroused in the hearts of the credulous (including some scientists and the BBC) gave Geller's activities immense publicity. Sober magicians familiar with the art of misdirection and the use of secret assistants had little doubt about his methods. Some (notably James Randi) were tireless and merciless in their exposures, which were justified in view of Geller's pretensions, though his skill and charm remain unquestioned. A reference to 'Gellerism' can be a useful lead-in to tricks with spoons, watches, etc. See Randi, THE MAGIC OF URI GELLER (1975).

'Gen, The'. magazines, magical.

'Genii'. magazines, magical.

Germain, Karl (Charles Mattmueller, 1878–1959). American magician of German parentage. His stage name was taken from the eighteenth-century man of mystery, Saint-Germain, and in some posters is spelt with an e at the end. From 1898 to 1905 he performed all over America and Canada, and was in Britain, including St George's Hall,

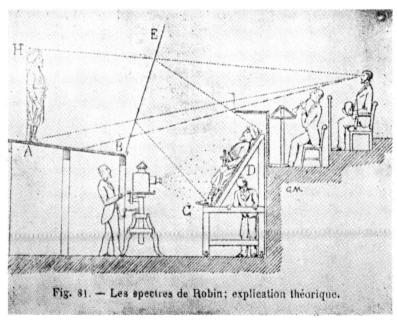

Fig. 81. — Les spectres de Robin; explication théorique.

74. Pepper's Ghost Trick.

1905–7. Soon afterwards he gave up magic for the law, but lost his sight and remained blind for 40 years. See Stuart Cramer, SECRETS OF KARL GERMAIN (1962), GERMAIN THE WIZARD AND HIS LEGERDEMAIN (1966).

Ghost Trick. Optical illusion in which ghosts apparently appeared on the stage with living actors, who could thrust a sword through the ghost without affecting it. The illusion was produced by an angled sheet of glass (at the front of the stage) which reflected a person hidden in the orchestra pit. A powerful light directed towards him caused the ghost to appear; *illustration 74.* The ghost was invisible to an actor on the stage, who had to direct his movements according to a prearranged plan. The ghost illusion was popularized and patented (in collaboration with Henry Dircks) by *J. H. Pepper* of the Regent Street Polytechnic, where the ghost was first shown in 1862. The principle involved was later used in various other illusions. *Robin.*

ghost tube. *phantom tube.*

Giant Memory. Feat involving genuine memorizing, though there is also a secret. Begin by learning a list of objects up to about 20, each object preferably having some connection with the number. For example, 'wand' = 1 (similar shape), 'bicycle' = 2 (two wheels), 'beehive' = 5 (rhymes), etc. When the list is complete it must be thoroughly memorized. Different spectators are asked to suggest an object for each number up to 20. As soon as the object is named you form a mental picture of it in association with *your* object. Thus if 'aeroplane' was named for 1, 'pig' for 2, 'dinner-plate' for 5, you might

picture an aeroplane balanced on a wand, a pig riding a bicycle, and a plate spinning on top of a beehive. It will be found easy to recall the correct object for numbers named at random by spectators. See Lamb, *MENTAL MAGIC*, pp.34–7; Devant, *THE BEST TRICKS*, pp.108–19.

Gibson, Walter B. American magical writer, perhaps the most prolific of all time. He began his career in the service of such legendary figures as *Thurston* and *Blackstone*, and was responsible for magic books published under their names. A close friend of *Houdini*: wrote *HOUDINI'S ESCAPADES* (1930), *HOUDINI'S MAGIC* (1932), from the magician's own notes. Other magic books include *THE WORLD'S BEST BOOK OF MAGIC* (1927), *PROFESSIONAL MAGIC FOR AMATEURS* (1948), *WHAT'S NEW IN MAGIC* (1957), *SECRETS OF THE GREAT MAGICIANS* (1967), *THE COMPLETE ILLUSTRATED BOOK OF CARD MAGIC* (1969). Also a writer on the occult, and of mystery stories under the name Maxwell Grant.

gimmick. Piece of equipment unseen and unsuspected by the audience but used in the performance of a trick (e.g. *thumb-writer*). The word is occasionally and less correctly used as a verb meaning to *fake*.

glass of water inverted. A glass or cup full of water can be turned upside down without the water escaping if a piece of stiff paper is first placed over the brim, owing to air pressure. By secretly fitting a circular piece of glass or plastic the exact size of the brim while adjusting the paper, the latter can then be safely slid away. The principle is used in some versions of the *Rice Bowls*.

glass of water vanished. A glass of water is placed on a box on the con-

75. Anti-gravity glasses on a plastic stick, shown by Edwin Hooper.

jurer's table and covered with a large handkerchief or small tea-cloth. The glass is now carried away and vanished. A ring the same size as the glass brim is sewn inside the handkerchief (a double one), and it is this ring which is lifted, while with his free hand the performer secretly lowers the glass out of sight behind the box or on to a *servante*. A *black art* well in the table can be used instead.

Glasses, Anti-gravity. A handkerchief is wrapped round a book or piece of board, and two or three glass tumblers are placed mouth downward on it. The book is now turned over but the glasses remain suspended. They are gripped, in fact, by an unseen *gimmick*. In one version the glasses are placed on a stick of plastic instead of a book; *illustration 75*. See Robinson, *MAGIC AS A PASTIME*, pp.85–7.

glide. To draw back the bottom card with the finger and take the next card instead; *illustration 76*.

glimpse. To note a card secretly, usually the bottom card, less often the top card. The performer must not be seen obviously looking at the

76. The glide, with bottom card drawn back. The hand has been raised to reveal the action for illustration purposes.

card. Natural glimpsing can often be achieved when receiving back a pack from a spectator after shuffling, or when the performer himself is casually shuffling the pack.

Golden Age of Magic. Term sometimes applied to a period of roughly 40 years, 1890–1930, when the big magic shows were a regular and accepted part of social entertainment. This was the period of *Devant*, the *Maskelynes, Chung Ling Soo, Le Roy, Lafayette, Goldin, Charlton, Selbit, Williams, Carmo, Morritt, Thurston, Houdini*, and other great magical names. In a typical week at least two dozen well-known magicians would be appearing in theatres or music halls in London and the provinces, as well as many lesser known conjurers, ventriloquists, and jugglers. The arrival of sound in the cinema about 1930 began the slow decline of the variety theatre, and TV hastened the process, aided by the curious popularity of Bingo. *history of magic.*

Goldfish Bowls. Old production trick, probably Chinese in origin, featured by *Phillippe* in Chinese costume, and subsequently by many later magicians. A shawl is thrown over the performer's arm, and from under it is brought a glass bowl containing water and goldfish. The feat is usually repeated two or three times. The bowls, fitted with rubber covers, are secreted in loading pockets within the performer's clothes.

Goldfish Catching. *fish-catching.*

Goldin, Horace (Hyman Goldstein, 1873–1939). Polish illusionist who went to live in America as a youth. His earliest attempts as a professional performer were handicapped by imperfect English, and he developed a new style of presenta-

tion, rushing through his programme at such speed that he became known as 'The Whirlwind Illusionist'. As such he set a new trend. He also called himself 'Royal Illusionist', though many other magicians also performed before various monarchs; *illustration 77.* His version of *Sawing a Woman in Half* was the most famous of his many notable tricks. Not long before his death he brought out an interesting autobiography, *IT'S FUN TO BE FOOLED* (1938).

Goldston, Will (1878–1948). Prominent figure in the magic world during the first three decades of the century. In his early years he performed under the name Carl Devo. He was manager of *Gamage's* magic department 1905–14, after which he opened his own magic shop at Aladdin House, 14 Green Street (now Irving Street). First editor of Gamage's *MAGICIAN MONTHLY*, editor of *THE MAGAZINE OF MAGIC* and of the *MAGICIAN ANNUAL* (1907–12), now collectors' items. Author of many conjuring text-books of varying quality, often well illustrated; the first was *SECRETS OF MAGIC* (1903), the last *TRICKS OF THE MASTERS* (1942), one of his best. The locks on his *EXCLUSIVE MAGICAL SECRETS* (1912) and its sequels (1921, 1927) were hardly justified by the contents, though these are by no means without interest. A paperback edition of the first is now available (1977). He was the founder of *THE MAGICIAN'S CLUB* (1911–39).

Goodliffe (C. Goodliffe Neale). A leading figure in the present magic world, who performed regularly in the Midlands before the last war. His outstanding contribution to magic, however, has been the found-

73

77. Caricature of Horace Goldin,
'Royal Illusionist'. In the background
are tiepins presented to him by the
Prince of Wales (George V), King
Edward VII, and the Queen of Saxony.
('Magician Annual'.)

78. Goodliffe.

American *close-up* performers and a maker of magical apparatus. His close-up show, performed to tape-recorded music, includes a *running gag* in which coins keep appearing under a salt-cellar.

Gozinta Boxes. Two boxes each of which fits inside the other, so that either one is alternately inside box and outside box, to the confusion of the audience. Obtainable from *Supreme Magic*; *illustration 79.*

79. Gozinta Boxes.

ing and editing of the weekly magical periodical *ABRACADABRA* (*ABRA* for short). His activities have given him an unrivalled knowledge of the magic scene and have taken him to 37 different countries. For almost every issue he has written a substantial editorial marked by individuality, integrity, and ripe experience. Also publisher of many excellent magic books, one of them his own *SIMPLY WIZARD* (1946). *Illustration 78.*

Good Night banner. A favourite way of closing a performance is to present a small black cloth which at command reveals the words 'Good Night' embroidered in a bright colour. They are on the inside of a flap allowed to fall at the right moment.

Goshman, Al. One of the leading

Grandmother's Necklace. Old trick with three large wooden beads and two lengths of string which hang together over the performer's arm. The beads are apparently threaded on to the middle of the two strings. Actually these strings are not side by side as they appear to be; they have been joined together in the middle by a piece of cotton, and when the beads are slipped on to the two ends at A (*illustration 80*) these are in fact the two ends of the same string. When the beads come to the middle they effectively hide the cotton join. An end from A and an end from B are taken and tied in a knot around the beads; *illustration 81*. This seemingly makes them more secure, but in fact when the ends at A and B are

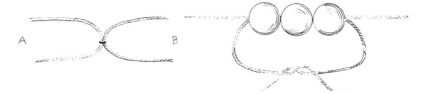

80. Grandmother's necklace: strings in middle.

81. Grandmother's necklace; knot tied around beads.

firmly pulled the beads drop off. Many variations of the principle have been used, with rings, cotton reels, etc. *Ropes and Rings*. See Lamb, *YOUR BOOK OF TABLE TRICKS*, pp.59–60. Hugard, *MODERN MAGIC MANUAL*, pp.276–80.

'Greater Magic'. Classic but advanced conjuring textbook by J. N. Hilliard, a journalist who was responsible for *Downs' ART OF MAGIC* (1909) and who joined the *Thurston* show in 1925. When he died suddenly in 1935 his unpublished writings were edited and illustrated respectively by *Hugard* and *Tarbell*, and published by Carl W. Jones in 1938 as a huge book (1006 pp.) covering the whole field of magic, with a stress on playing-cards; a valuable book now expensive and hard to procure.

Gun Trick. *Bullet Catch.*

H

Hall, Trevor H., M.A., Ph.D. Remarkably versatile, Dr Hall has been chartered surveyor, director of a building society, lecturer in bibliography, and skilful conjurer, besides being an authority on old conjuring books, psychic research, and Sherlock Holmes. His earliest books deal expertly with sleight-of-hand (e.g. *THE TESTAMENT OF RALPH W. HULL*, 1945; *NOTHING IS IMPOSSIBLE*, 1946). Later, some-times in collaboration, he wrote some outstanding critical works on supposed psychic matters (e.g. *THE SPIRITUALISTS*, 1962; *THE STRANGE CASE OF EDMUND GURNEY*, 1964; *NEW LIGHT ON OLD GHOSTS*, 1965). *OLD CONJURING BOOKS* (1972) is of great interest to the collector. *bibliographies*; *Harry Price*.

Hamley's. Longest established firm dealing in magic, first opened in 1760. Took over the magical shop of

Joseph Bland, a well-known Victorian magic dealer, at the turn of the century. The main branch has long been in Regent Street, London. Hamley's have issued many fine magic catalogues. *dealers.*

hand magic. *sleight-of-hand.*

handcuff escapes. May be performed in various ways, including the use of trick handcuffs. Where genuine cuffs are used, the escaper may carry with him keys of various makes, if necessary employing an extension holder or gripping them in his teeth. Some cuffs can be opened merely with a sharp blow, while others yield to a simple piece of wire. *escapology*; *Houdini.* See Gibson, *HOUDINI ESCAPES*, pp.11–14; Houdini, *HANDCUFF SECRETS* (1910).

handkerchief ball. *Gimmick* for producing or vanishing *silks.* A small flesh-coloured ball with a hole in one side is supplied with a thumb-loop of invisible thread, etc., so that it can be secretly swung behind the palm, and the hands then shown apparently empty. Some adroitness is needed to use it effectively. Another form of ball has no loop and is kept concealed by sleight-of-hand. *Stillwell ball.*

Handkerchief, Dancing. *Dancing Handkerchief.*

Handkerchief, Demon. Large handkerchief used for vanishing small articles. It is formed by sewing two similar handkerchiefs together, and in the middle of one of them making a slit big enough to take a watch or similar object. This is apparently wrapped in the handkerchief but really slipped through the slit, and the handkerchief can be opened out to show that the watch is missing. See Scarne, *SCARNE'S MAGIC TRICKS*, pp.182–3; Hoffmann, *MODERN MAGIC*, p.195.

handkerchief production. A single handkerchief may be *balled* and *stolen* from armpit or elbow (after the hands have been shown empty) under the guise of pulling up the sleeves. Or it may be obtained from a partly open matchbox in the act of lighting a candle, the *silk* being seemingly snatched from the flame. Or a false *finger* or *handkerchief ball* may be used. A batch of silks may be loaded into a hat or box from a *servante* or from under the jacket, or a *production box* may be used. A *mirror glass* is another possibility. See Hugard, *MODERN MAGIC MANUAL*, pp.182–7.

handkerchief through leg. Old parlour trick, the principle of which is still sometimes used on the modern stage. The middle of a large twisted handkerchief is placed against the front of the leg, and the two ends appear to be passed right round the leg and brought to the front to be knotted. In fact, instead of crossing over behind the leg, each half is bent into a loop, and two loops are slip-

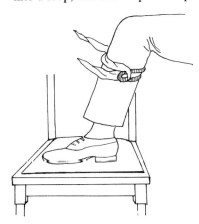

82. Handkerchief pulled through leg. One loop is shaded in the picture to make it clearer.

ped one into the other, and each end is brought back to the front on the same side as before; see *illustration 82*. A pull on the knot makes it appear that the handkerchief has been drawn right through the leg. The neck may be substituted for the leg.

handkerchief vanish. A single handkerchief may be vanished by sleight-of-hand after being *balled*; by a *pull*; by a *cone*; with a *handkerchief ball* or *Stillwell ball*; or in various other ways. A *false finger* may be used, being secretly enclosed in the left hand, opening upward. The handkerchief is openly pushed into the closed fist but actually enters the finger, which is then carried away attached to the right hand.

handkerchief wand. Apparatus for vanishing a handkerchief. It is hollow and contains a rod that is allowed to slip secretly into a cone (or long envelope). A handkerchief is openly placed within this and is secretly draped over the rod. The wand ostensibly pokes the handkerchief down into the bottom of the cone, but actually it is pushed completely over the rod and handkerchief, drawing these away when it is removed.

Harbin, Robert (Ned Williams, 1910–78). Brilliant magical inventor and illusionist. Born in South Africa, he came to London as a youth. After working with concert

83. Robert Harbin as stage illusionist.

parties and as salesman at *Gamage's*, he was engaged at *Maskelyne*'s Home of Mystery, where the presence of *Oswald Williams* necessitated Ned's adopting a pseudonym. The most famous of his many clever inventions was the *Zig-Zag Girl*, in which a girl in a cabinet has her middle part visibly pushed away from the rest of her. Harbin exposed many of his ingenious tricks in *THE MAGIC OF ROBERT HARBIN* (1970), but the number of copies was strictly limited, the price exceptionally high, and each purchaser had to sign an agreement not to divulge the book's secrets. Harbin was generally accepted as the leading magician of his generation, and he was undoubtedly the most prolific magical inventor since *Selbit*. He was also an expert on *Origami*, on which he wrote several books. *Illustration 83*.

Hardeen, Theo (Theodore Weiss, 1876–1944). Brother of *Houdini*, performing a double act with him until Houdini's marriage. Then, with his brother's encouragement, Theo toured with a similar escape act to that of Houdini, though he never achieved the same dramatic flair.

Hartz, Joseph Michael (1836–1903). English-born conjurer of Dutch descent who settled in America after a successful debut in England. His reputation was based particularly on his use of crystal apparatus and on his remarkable *hat production* routine, known as The Devil of a Hat. Though much admired by fellow magicians for his skill and subtlety, he was said to lack showmanship. None the less he received many honours from royalty in Europe and elsewhere. *Hoffmann* gave a detailed analysis of his work in *MAGICAL TITBITS* (1911).

hat productions. A top hat was at one time a favourite object from which to produce various articles magically, including cannon balls, cabbages, bird cages, lighted chinese lanterns, balloons, *spring flowers*, etc. Nowadays boxes and tubes are more often used for *productions*. Hartz's Devil of a Hat was the greatest feat of its kind ever performed: the hat production, carried out in silence, lasted for nearly half an hour, and included a skull which rose from the hat on its own; *illustration 84*.

84. Hartz's Devil of a Hat (Hoffmann, 'Magical Titbits'.)

heap. Word often used for a packet of cards cut or dealt from the main pack.

Heller, Robert (William Henry Palmer, c.1830–78). Born in Canterbury, England (where his father was an organist) and trained as a musician. Seeing a show given by *Robert-Houdin* created a desire to be a similar magician. Early efforts failed, despite a wig and a French

85. Herrmann at the Egyptian Hall.

accent. After falling back on music as a career he adopted a fresh magical style, mixing magic, music, and humour, and was highly successful in America. Returning to London, he teamed up with a girl (presented as his sister) in a *second-sight* act that became a leading feature of his performance.

Henning, Douglas. Canadian magician who made a great success in New York in a magical-musical show, *THE MAGIC SHOW* (1974). The thin plot, about a has-been magician unsuccessfully trying to spoil the act of a young one (Henning), serves as vehicle for some well-presented illusions. Henning, modern in attire, soft-voiced and sincere in manner, shows good dramatic sense and provides a real air of mystery.

Herrmann, Alexander (1843–96). Prominent American magician, though born in France of German parents. He began his career with an elder brother, Carl (or Compars), but later branched out on his own. With his little goatee beard and heavy black moustache he typified the popular idea of a magician; showmanship and publicity made him the best-known performer of his day. In Britain he gave over 1,000 performances at the *Egyptian Hall* (1870–2); *illustration 85*. After his death his wife Adelaide and nephew Leon carried on with his act, but never succeeded in replacing him.

Hertz, Carl (Leib or Louis Morganstern, 1859–1924). American illusionist who toured widely but settled in England. He looked the part of a magician but was only an average performer, though his magical career was a long one. His two most famous tricks were *De Kolta's Vanishing Lady* and *Bird-cage Van-*

ish. The latter was performed with some cruelty despite Hertz's pretence to the contrary, including a performance before an easily duped House of Commons committee in 1921.

Hey Presto! Term of command sometimes used by conjurers in a vanishing or transformation trick. The musical term *presto* means 'quickly'. See *magic words*.

Hilliard, J. N. *GREATER MAGIC*.

Hindu shuffle. Rather similar to an *overhand shuffle* but with the cards held at the long sides instead of the short sides. Like the overhand, it can be used as a *false shuffle*.

history of magic. No one knows when magic first began, but it has close links with the religion and the simple medicine of primitive man. The first record of magic as an entertainment relates to a performance about 5,000 years ago by *Dedi*, an Egyptian. There are Biblical references to Egyptian magicians competing with Aaron. Roman priests used magic in their temples to awe their congregations. In medieval times *jugglers* (i.e. conjurers) performed at fairgrounds and market-places, and sometimes in noblemen's halls. But although a few notable conjurers, such as *Pinetti*, achieved distinction before 1800, in the main conjuring remained a fairground entertainment until well on in the nineteenth century, when the conjurer (represented by such men as *Anderson*, *Robert-Houdin*, *Maskelyne*, and *Bertram*) became a respected figure in society. Perhaps the greatest days of magic were c.1890–1914, when, in addition to the *Home of Mystery*, variety theatres all over the country were constantly open to magicians, and famous magical names such as *Chung Ling Soo*, *Goldin*, *Downs*,

Houdini, De Biere, Lafayette, and many others, could be seen on playbills every week of the year. By the end of World War II a change was taking place. Variety theatres were closing, and the big magic shows became fewer. Today magic remains very popular – there are more people practising it than ever before – but it is more often seen in clubs, cabarets, cruise ships, and at parties than on the stages of large theatres. TV, which has indirectly helped to close the variety theatres, has at the same time helped to give a boost to public interest in magic, particularly with such shows as those presented by *David Nixon* in Britain and by *Mark Wilson* in the U.S.A. *Golden Age*.

The first history of magic as an entertainment was *Frost*'s LIVES OF THE CONJURERS (1876). Not for nearly another 50 years was another significant history produced: Clarke's ANNALS OF CONJURING (1924–8). Other useful histories published since then are *Evans*'s HISTORY OF CONJURING AND MAGIC (1930), *Mulholland*'s STORY OF MAGIC (1935), Dexter's THIS IS MAGIC (1958), Lamb's PEGASUS BOOK OF MAGICIANS (1967), and *Christopher*'s splendid PANORAMA OF MAGIC (1962) and ILLUSTRATED HISTORY OF MAGIC (1973). *Houdini*'s UNMASKING OF ROBERT-HOUDIN contains interesting historical material. *100 YEARS OF MAGIC POSTERS* by C. and R. Reynolds (1976) offers attractive pictorial records, very well annotated. See also *Dawes*.

hocus pocus. Term formerly applied to conjuring, probably deriving from a mock-solemn nonsense phrase uttered by a seventeenth-century *juggler* to impress spectators. The term became used to indicate a conjurer himself, as well as his art. A derivation from the Latin words used at Mass, '*hoc est corpus*', has been suggested, but remains doubtful.

'Hocus Pocus Junior'. Title of the first illustrated English book devoted solely to conjuring (1634). Many of the tricks were taken from *Scot*, but the book also contained new ones. Among the tricks included were the *Grandmother's Necklace* and the magic *funnel*.

Hoffmann, Professor Louis (Angelo Lewis, 1839–1919). Famous English writer on magic, a barrister and journalist by profession. His interest in magic led him to write a series of conjuring articles for Routledge's EVERY BOY'S MAGAZINE. These were expanded into a book, *MODERN MAGIC* (1876), which has had more influence on the art of conjuring than any other book, and which ran into 18 editions. It taught magic to thousands of readers, and by explaining (perhaps too extensively) the secrets of almost all known tricks and illusions, it indirectly encouraged the invention of new ones. Three later books, *MORE MAGIC* (1890), *LATER MAGIC* (1904), and *MAGICAL TITBITS* (1911), supplemented *MODERN MAGIC*; he also wrote many other books on conjuring and games, and made useful translations of *Robert-Houdin*'s conjuring books. *CONJURER DICK*.

Hofzinser, Johann (1806–75). Brilliant Austrian conjurer, generally regarded as the founder of modern card magic.

Home of Mystery. Name used by *Maskelyne* for his theatres of magic at the *Egyptian Hall* and *St George's Hall*.

Hooper, Edwin. Prominent British magic dealer. After working as a Punch and Judy man on a Devon beach, he gained some experience with the magic dealer, Jack Hughes. Deciding later to set up his own business at his home town, Bideford, Devon, he borrowed £200, added his own savings, and founded the very successful *Supreme Magic Co.* His magical interests are wide, but he specializes in children's tricks. *Illustration 75.*

Houdini, Harry (Ehrich Weiss, 1874–1926). American illusionist noted chiefly for escape acts and publicity methods, and generally regarded as the greatest showman in magical history. Born in Hungary, the son of a Jewish rabbi, he was taken to America as a young child. Inspired by the writings of *Robert-Houdin*, he became a professional conjurer while still in his teens, partnered by his brother (*Hardeen*) and later by his wife, Bess. Success did not come until he specialized in rope and handcuff escapes. Genuine skill, experience, and vigorous publicity (including gaol escapes) made him a great star who became world-famous through his escapes from bank safes, strait-jackets and packing-cases lowered into rivers. He was an avid magical collector whose books are now in the Library of Congress. He died after a blow in the stomach from a careless student. *Illustrations 63, 148. escapology; UNMASKING OF ROBERT-HOUDIN.* See Gibson, *HOUDINI ESCAPES* (1930); Christopher, *HOUDINI, THE UNTOLD STORY* (1969), and *HOUDINI: A PICTORIAL LIFE* (1976); Gresham, *THE MAN WHO WALKED THROUGH WALLS* (1959). His own best book is *A MAGICIAN AMONG THE SPIRITS* (1924).

houlette. Holder for a pack of cards, often used with the *Rising Cards* and similar tricks. It may be elaborately ornamented, faked, or simply a plain holder of metal and glass or plastics; *illustration 86.*

86. Card houlette.

Hugard, Jean (John G. Boyce, 1872–1959). Australian magician who performed all over the world and settled in America. A feature of his act was the *Bullet Catch*. Later he made a great reputation as a teacher of conjuring and a writer on the technical side of magic. Many of his books are standard works, including *MODERN MAGIC MANUAL* (1939), *THE ROYAL ROAD TO CARD MAGIC* (with Frederick Braue, 1949), and *ENCYCLOPEDIA OF CARD TRICKS* (1937). For many years he edited and published a highly regarded journal, entitled *HUGARD'S MAGIC MONTHLY.* In spite of deafness and blindness, he remained one of the world's great authorities on magic until his death. *magazines, magical.*

83

I

I.B.M. *International Brotherhood of Magicians.*

illusion. Although any conjuring trick presents an illusion in one sense, the word is usually applied by magicians to large-scale tricks performed on a stage and involving a human being or large animal (e.g. *Asrah*, *Dizzy Limit*, *Lion's Bride*, etc.).

illusion, optical. *optical trick.*

impromptu trick. One that can be performed on the spur of the moment, without previous *preparation* or special apparatus (but *not* without *practice*).

index. *card index.*

Indian magic. Reputed to be very ancient, but Western conjurers who have visited India have generally found the repertoire limited. Perhaps the most impressive trick of the traditional Indian conjurers was the *Basket trick*. Other tricks popular in India have been the *Coloured Sands*, the *Ring on Stick*, the *Cups and Balls*, and the *Mango Tree Trick*. Indian fakirs have specialized in such feats as snake charming and burial alive. Some Indian magicians have become well-known in the West, among the most notable being the Indian jugglers who visited London early in the nineteenth century and *Sorcar* and his son after World War II. *Indian Rope Trick*; *indrajal*; *jadoo-wallah*; *fakir*.

Indian Rope Trick. Perhaps the most famous of all magical mysteries. Accounts vary, but basically a fakir throws up a long coil of rope into the air, where it remains rigid. A boy climbs up and refuses to come down, so the fakir goes up after him, carrying a knife. Presently he tosses down the boy's limbs, one by one; these are bundled into a basket, and the boy comes to life again. Unfortunately there is no convincing evidence supporting the existence of this miracle, descriptions of which are usually hearsay and invariably indicate confusion of mind and liveliness of imagination. Magicians and others who have searched India for a conjurer able to perform the trick (often offering substantial rewards) have failed to find any sign of it. The theory that spectators have been hypnotized into *thinking* that they saw it is as fantastic as the story itself. Attempts have been made, by *Thurston*, *Goldin*, and others, to reproduce the illusion on the stage, but with limited success. It has been plausibly argued that the Rope Trick is a legend connected with religious symbolism.

indifferent card. Any card other than that chosen by a spectator in the course of a trick, or any card whose value is of no significance.

indrajal. Indian term for magic.

Inexhaustible Bottle. Old trick (featured by *Anderson*, *Robert-Houdin*, etc.) in which a great many drinks of various kinds are poured from a single bottle. Although the bottle looks ordinary it is *faked*, being divided into several compartments, each containing a different drink. The flow of drinks is controlled by airholes covered by the performer's fingers. Sometimes an empty bottle is secretly switched for a full one. Kettles based on the same principle are also used.

Inexhaustible Box. Piece of apparatus used for *productions*. One form is so constructed that if the box is tipped forward any articles in it are automatically concealed. The true bottom of the box remains stationary, and a false bottom, previously lying against the front of the box, takes its place; *illustration 87*. Further objects can be secretly *loaded* from a *servante*.

International Brotherhood of Magicians (I.B.M.). Society founded in 1923 by a Canadian amateur magician, Len Vintus, and two American friends. From this small beginning there developed an organization that now stretches all over the world, though most of its 7,000 members are American. With head-quarters in Kenton, Ohio, it is divided into groups (known as Rings) according to areas. Most are based in the U.S.A., but there are also Rings in many other countries, including Great Britain (*British Ring*). The Brotherhood's monthly journal, *THE LINKING RING*, is one of the largest magical *magazines* in the world. Large conventions are held periodically in the U.S.A.

International Magic Studio. Well-known London magic dealers who began in 1960 and now have two shops and a studio, and are manufacturers and wholesalers to several other dealers. They publish a bi-monthly magazine, *MAGIC INFO*, edited by Harry Baron and issued from their office at 89 Clerkenwell Road, Holborn. The firm is run by Ron Macmillan, a clever sleight-of-hand performer. *Illustration 1*.

Ireland, Frances. *Marshall, Frances.*

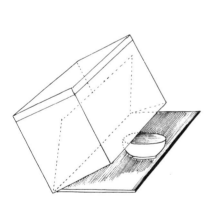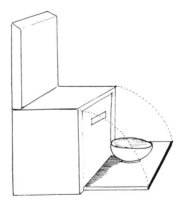

87. Inexhaustible box, showing bowl concealed by false bottom.

J

jadoo-wallah. Indian conjurer.

Jap Box. *Inexhaustible Box.* Nowadays usually applied to a lidless, bottomless box with compressible *loads* hidden in two rather thick sides. These have inner flaps which drop down, releasing the loads.

'Jinx'. American magical journal, produced by *Annemann*, and devoted mainly to *mentalism*. The first number was issued in 1934, and the last (no. 151) in 1941.

jog. To push a card or batch of cards slightly out of alignment when giving the pack an overhand shuffle, so as to be able to find it (them) again. To *injog* the card is to push it towards the performer. To *outjog* it is to push it away from him. *false shuffle.*

Johnson, George (1876–1962). Well-known magical journalist, editor of *THE MAGIC WAND* for many years, and responsible for the publication of numerous useful conjuring books and booklets. His own *CONJURERS' TALES* (1910) were fiction based on magical themes.

Johnson, Roy. Clever and amusing professional conjurer who gave many performances at the Windmill Theatre before becoming a club and cabaret performer. Depends largely upon subtlety for his effects, many of which have been carefully described in *THE ROY JOHNSON EXPERIENCE* (1970) and its sequels *SECOND TIME AROUND* (1971) and *THIRD DIMENSION* (1977).

journals, magical. *magazines, magical.*

juggler. Performer of non-deceptive feats of dexterity. *conjurer.*

jumbo cards. Extra large playing-cards suitable for use on the stage, sometimes known as Jumbos; *illustration 88.*

Just Chance. Popular trick which allows three or four spectators each to choose an envelope from a batch of four or five, the performer being left with the remaining one. His proves to hold (say) a £5 note. Theirs have each a card saying 'Bad luck!'. All the envelopes, in fact, are similar. The note, though apparently drawn from inside the performer's envelope, is really drawn from outside it, where it has been secreted. See Warlock, *COMPLETE BOOK OF MAGIC*, pp.51–4; Reed, *MAGICAL MIRACLES YOU CAN DO*, 58–9.

88. Jumbo card shown with normal cards.

K

Kalanag (Helmut Schreiber, 1893–1963). Portly German illusionist who adopted the name Kalanag (Black Snake) from Kipling's Jungle Book, in which it is the name of an elephant. Originally engaged in the film industry, he later developed a magic act. After the war his show was based on that of *Dante*, whose title *SIM SALA BIM* he also appropriated. In due course it became the largest and most spectacular magic revue of the post-war period, with his strikingly beautiful wife, Gloria, as the chief of many glamorous assistants. *Lota Vase.*

Kaps, Fred. Outstanding Dutch magician, generally regarded by most fellow conjurers as one of the supreme living performers. Formerly appeared under the name 'Mystico'. A versatile artist who hides his skill by making magic look easy. A feature of his act (often the close) is a prolonged pouring of salt from one hand.

Kellar, Harry (1849–1922). Notable American magician, in his early days assistant to the *Davenport Brothers* and to an old-time American magician, the Fakir of Ava. At length achieved success on his own through clever showmanship and assiduity. Many of his tricks were copied from more original performers such as *Maskelyne*, but his Davenport cabinet performance was outstanding. He travelled widely with his show, but in America an absurd rivalry with *Alexander Herrmann* at one time affected the prosperity of both men; each exposed the tricks of the other. When Herrmann died Kellar was left the leader of American magic. At his retirement he passed on his show to *Thurston*. His reminiscences, *A MAGICIAN'S TOUR*, appeared in 1896.

Kellar tie. Devised by Kellar for use in rope escapes. The basis was that after the left wrist had been tied, both wrists were fastened together behind the back, but in the process the performer secretly gathered a loop of slack rope and held it firmly against one wrist. No matter how tightly the rope was tied after this, the right hand could quickly slip free and replace itself at will. See Hatton and Plate, *MAGICIANS' TRICKS*, pp.292–7.

kettle, magic. *Inexhaustible Bottle.*

key card. Card indicating a chosen card which has been seemingly *lost* in the pack. The bottom card acts as a key card if it is secretly glimpsed before the return of the chosen card to the top of the pack. However many times the cards are cut, the chosen card will remain the one immediately following the glimpsed key card when the cards are dealt. *Thick, slick, long,* and *short* cards may also be used as key cards.

Kio, Emil (1900–65). Famous Russian magician who performed big illusions in the middle of a circus arena. Among his most striking effects were a cremation trick (a girl standing on a table was hidden by a curtain which was then set ablaze) and the transformation of a caged

87

woman to a caged lion. After Emil's death the Kio show was effectively continued by his son, Igor.

Knight's Tour. *Mentalism* feat, which may be shown as a feat of memory. The squares on a chessboard (which in performance may be drawn on a blackboard) are numbered horizontally, starting at top left, from 1 to 64. The problem is for an imaginary chess knight to visit every square, moving correctly, without landing on any square twice, and starting on any square suggested. The performer may turn his back (or be blindfolded) as he calls out the numbers, which a spectator marks on the blackboard. The correct sequence is:

60, 45, 39, 29, 12, 6, 16, 31, 37, 20, 26, 36, 30, 13, 28, 38, 53, 43, 33, 27, 44, 61, 55, 40, 23, 8, 14, 24, 7, 22, 5, 15, 32, 47, 64, 54, 48, 63, 46, 56, 62, 52, 58, 41, 51, 57, 42, 59, 49, 34, 17, 2, 19, 9, 3, 18, 1, 11, 21, 4, 10, 25, 35, 50 (then 60, etc.)

The numbers can be written on a small card and tucked (say) in the wrist-watch strap to be secretly consulted.

knife force. Also known as a slip or backslip force. A spectator inserts a knife somewhere in a pack of cards, and the performer openly makes a *break* there. As he lifts off the upper half with one hand the fingers of his other hand slip the top card (to be forced) to the top of the lower heap, and this card is taken by the spectator. See Clive, *CARD TRICKS WITHOUT SKILL*, p.33; Hugard and Braue, *ROYAL ROAD TO CARD MAGIC*, pp.121–2.

knots. *Silks* and ropes are most commonly used in knot tricks. Tying a knot with one hand is an old impromptu handkerchief trick; it can be done even better with soft string or a bootlace. Another old knot trick is taking an end in each hand and tying a knot without releasing either end. (It can be done by folding the arms first.) A handkerchief knot tied by a spectator can be converted to a fake knot by grasping a corner above and below the knot and then pulling. A knot can be made to untie itself magically by the use of thread. The *cut and restored rope* is sometimes combined with knot tricks. See Hay, *AMATEUR MAGICIAN'S HANDBOOK*, pp.252–9; Baron, *CLOSE-UP MAGIC FOR BEGINNERS*, pp.133–7; Hugard, *MODERN MAGIC MANUAL*, pp.205–10; Gibson, *PROFESSIONAL MAGIC FOR AMATEURS*, pp.131–50.

Koran, Al (Edward Doe, 1916–72). Famous British *mentalist*, who started his working career as a hairdresser before turning to magic. At first he concentrated on card and close-up conjuring, but his dignified presence allied to subtle thinking brought him fame in mental magic, especially on TV. In 1969 he decided to try his fortune in the U.S.A., where he died three years later. A book to which his name was attached, *BRING OUT THE MAGIC IN YOUR MIND* (1964), is best forgotten, *PROFESSIONAL PRESENTATIONS* (1968), however, lives up to its title. *AL KORAN'S LEGACY* (1973) was posthumous. Both books were written by Hugh Miller.

Kovari, George (Gyuri Kovari). Hungarian who came to England over 20 years ago at the age of 18 and has settled here ever since as a professional magician and dealer. He frequently offers a full-length magic act most attractively presented, marked by a style that is both informal and impressive, providing magic in the manner of the *Golden Age* without pretension or pomposity.

Kreskin (George Kresge). *Mentalist* in the style of *Dunninger* but with a lighter touch. TV appearances helped to put him on the map, both in America and in Britain. His performances include mental feats, muscle reading, and suggestion, which in effect is very close to hypnotism. Though he rightly disclaims supernatural or psychic powers and criticizes those who pretend to such faculties, he is less critical regarding telepathy. A skilful conjurer, especially with cards. He has told his story in THE AMAZING WORLD OF KRESKIN (1973). *Illustration 89.*

89. Kreskin in merry mood.

L

Lafayette (Sigmund Neuberger, 1872–1911). Eccentric German-born American illusionist who gave many sensational performances in the U.S.A. and Britain. He was essentially a showman, with a limited knowledge of magic as an art, but he had a remarkable sense of the dramatic, and his shows attracted great attention. He started his main career with a barefaced imitation of *Ching Ling Foo* and several dazzlingly quick changes of costume, then broadened his act with some daring illusions in which big animals often featured, such as the Lion's Bride. His treatment of these creatures could be callous, but his affection for his dogs, particularly his favourite, Beauty, was abnormal; she had her own private suite, with porcelain bathtub. He lost his life when an Edinburgh theatre was burnt down during a performance.

lapping. The art of using the lap as a *servante* when seated at a table. To do this effectively requires good *misdirection*, and the audience must be seated directly opposite the performer. See Ganson, THE MAGIC OF SLYDINI, Chaps. 1 & 2.

Leat, Harry (1874–1949). Magic dealer noted for his forthrightness. His *LEAFLETS*, periodically issued free to customers (1925–40), expressed his views on magical topics with pugnacious candour, his especial targets being (1) *exposure* and (2) the ill-treatment of animals in magic. Before working on his own he was for many years in charge of Ornum's magic store; his experiences and encounters are brightly and bluntly related in *FORTY YEARS IN AND AROUND MAGIC* (1923). He issued several other books printed and published by himself.

legerdemain. Strictly speaking, sleight-of-hand, but more often used of conjuring generally, especially up to the mid-nineteenth century.

Leipzig, Nate (1873–1939). American magician born in Stockholm. Began his working life as an optician, but his interest in magic at length drew him to turn professional. Although essentially a sleight-of-hand performer, he was successful on the music-hall stage. His great reputation as a manipulator, however, came from his close-up work at private engagements and among fellow conjurers.

Le Roy, Servais (1865–1953). Belgian-born illusionist, who was brought up in England but afterwards settled in America. A clever inventor as well as a capable performer, among whose most notable originations were the levitation illusion *Asrah* and a Devil's Cage from which he was able to vanish instantly despite its examination by a committee. At one time he performed in a trio with Imro Fox and F. E. Powell, two well-known American conjurers; later, and more permanently, as leader of another trio, consisting of himself, his English wife known as Talma, and a magical comedian named Bosco.

Levante, Les (Leslie George Cole, 1892–1978). Australian illusionist who toured the world as The Great Levante with his show 'How's Tricks?', visiting Britain more than once. An excellent showman with an engaging manner, noted for his friendliness on and off the stage, Levante presented an attractive and varied magical entertainment. The highlight was perhaps the convincing presentation of his steel *Substitution Trunk* (sometimes with his daughter Esmé), which stood in the lobby of the theatre before the performance for anyone to examine. He officially retired in 1955 but made several later appearances.

levitation. Rising into the air (the opposite of gravitation); an effective feat with both objects and living persons; *illustration 57*. It should not be confused with *aerial suspension*, where some visible contact with the ground is maintained. *J. N. Maskelyne* first introduced levitation in 1873, his wife floating up from the stage horizontally. A few months afterwards he himself (really a dummy) appeared to float vertically, right above the auditorium; *illustration 98*. Since then many magicians have levitated their assistants in many different ways, two of the most popular being *Aga* and *Asrah*; *illustrations 90, 91*. In America Kellar made a great feature in 1904 of 'The Levitation of Princess Karnac', which was really Maskelyne's old illusion. Inanimate objects, from handkerchiefs and *floating balls* to an electric organ (*Calvert*), have been freely encouraged to ignore the law of gravitation. One of the most effective is Norm

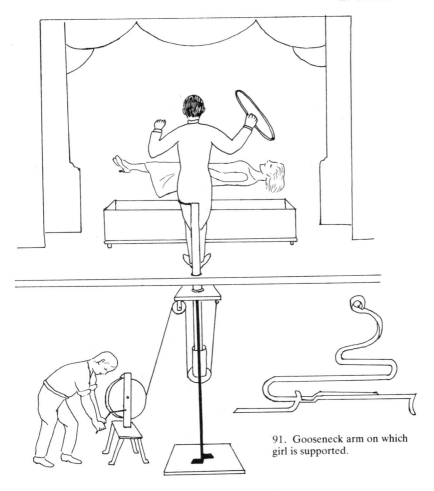

90. 'Aga' levitation, with rod hidden by magician's body.

91. Gooseneck arm on which girl is supported.

Nielsen's floating violin, which plays as it floats. Threads, wires, and other gimmicks have all been used in levitations. *Zombie*.

Lewis, Angelo. Professor Louis Hoffmann, 1839–1919.

lie detection. Interesting finish to a card trick. A spectator who has selected a card is shown the shuffled cards one by one and asked to say 'Not mine' to all, including his own. He is told that his lie will be detected through tone of voice, shifty eyes, etc. The performer in fact knows the card through a *key card* or a *one-way* pattern: the lie detection is misdirection. Many variations are possible. See Elliott, *MAGIC: 100 NEW TRICKS*, pp.110–11.

Light and Heavy Chest. A favourite trick of *Robert-Houdin*, devised by himself. Spectators were invited to lift a box by its handle. When he willed them to do so they had no difficulty, but if he willed them not to, they failed. The secret was the passing of an electrical magnetic force to the box, so powerful that it could withstand any human effort. He used this very effectively on his Algerian visit.

'Linking Ring, The'. Journal of the *I.B.M.*

Linking Rings. An old trick performed by Chinese magicians at least 150 years ago, but still a standard trick performed by many tip-top conjurers. The basic routine is the showing of (usually) eight metal rings, about 21 cm (8 or 9 in) in diameter, all apparently separate. The performer then proceeds to link them together in various ways; *illustration 92*. Finally they are counted again as seemingly separate rings. A set of rings (procurable from most

92. Linking rings.

magic dealers) often consists of two unfaked separate rings, two linked together, three linked together, and one ring with a tiny gap in it. The whole art of the trick lies in the performer's ability to make his handling of the rings convincing, smooth, and entertaining. There are many different routines, some of them varying the number of rings used. *Three-ring Routine.* See Hugard, *MODERN MAGIC MANUAL*, pp.169–76; Hay, *AMATEUR MAGICIAN'S HANDBOOK*, pp.281–6.

Lion's Bride. Sensational illusion presented by Lafayette. A girl dressed as a bride entered the cage of a genuine roaring lion, which reared up on its hind legs and sprang – only to be revealed as Lafayette himself in lion's costume. An unseen *switch* with the real lion was made by a revolving panel.

'Lives of the Conjurers'. *Frost.*

Livestock. Some spectators enjoy the mysterious appearances and disappearances of birds and animals. Others strongly dislike the magician's use of living creatures as if they were cards or billiard balls, and are apt to take an unfavourable view of the performer who uses them. The secretary of the R.S.P.C.A. wrote a few years ago: 'Today the public is quite sophisticated, and there is a growing fear that tricks where animals and birds are used are only possible by the confining of them in cramped spaces.' This fear has never really been resolved. *animals in magic.*

Living and Dead Test. Popular mental feat. Several spectators are each given a slip of paper. The first is asked to write the name of someone (unknown to the performer) who is no longer alive. The rest each write a living person's name (also unknown). The slips are folded and mixed together. When the performer opens and reads them he unfailingly picks out the dead name, no matter how the various handwritings are disguised. The secret is that the slip given to the first person is torn from the top of a sheet of writing paper, and thus has one long smooth edge. The other slips all have two rough edges. (The bottom slip is not used.) The trick may be varied in a number of ways. Some conjurers feel that the theme is rather a morbid one for entertainment, and they substitute, for example, male and female initials,

93. Lota vase.

or real and imaginary people. See Lamb, *YOUR BOOK OF MENTAL MAGIC*, p.23; Baron, *CLOSE-UP MAGIC FOR BEGINNERS*, p.40; Ganson, *MAGIC OF THE MIND*, pp.38–43.

load. One or more articles to be secretly introduced into a container (e.g. hat or box) for subsequent *production*. The load is usually hidden behind some larger article on the table, or on a *servante*, or in the magician's clothing. To load an article is to introduce it secretly into the container.

locator card. One specially made, treated, or *glimpsed* so that it can easily be found by touch or sight: e.g. *long card*, *upside-down card*,

thick card. It is most often used to locate a *selected card* by being placed next to it. *key card.*

long card. *Locator card* fractionally longer than the rest of the pack and thus easily found by touch. It is also easy to cut at a long card.

lost. Term applied to a card chosen by a spectator and then shuffled into the pack so that its position cannot be known either to the performer or to anyone else.

Lota Vase. Vessel from which water can be repeatedly poured although it appears empty at the end of each pouring. There are many styles and sizes. The top of the vase leads to an inner cylinder with a slot at the bottom. The whole vase is completely filled, and if the water in the cylinder is poured out, the vase will then appear empty. But water in the outer chamber will gradually pass through the slot into the cylinder until it finds its own level. The process is repeated until the whole vase is empty. The Lota is sometimes used as a *running gag*. The name derives from an Indian word for a water vessel. *Illustration 93.*

Lyle, Cecil (1892–1955). British magician known at one time as 'The Magical Milliner', as he made a feature of tricks with ladies' hats. A trick in which torn-up pieces of tissue were restored in the form of a paper hat was very widely copied. He performed frequently with *Maskelyne*; later he bought *Goldin*'s show and calling himself 'The Great Lyle' offered a big illusion show under the name 'Cavalcade of Mystery'. In addition to the Goldin tricks there were others by *Devant*, *Williams*, etc. His performance usually included an item entitled 'Lyle's Marvellous Hands', in which he performed sleight-of-hand tricks with smoothness and skill.

Lynn, Dr H. S. (Hugh Simmons, 1836–99). Eminent magician of the later Victorian period. Starting his career in the navy, he first became a professional conjurer in Australia, then went to America. Here he claimed to have taken a medical degree, but he continued to tour as a professional conjurer. He was noted for his gift of the gab and his humorous manner. His tricks were often followed by a spoof explanation of 'How It's Done'. Among his most notable tricks were the *Box Trick*, and a trick (*Palingenesia*) in which a man's arms, legs, and head were apparently cut off. He told his story in *THE ADVENTURES OF THE STRANGE MAN* (1873), repeating it in *TRAVELS AND ADVENTURES OF DR LYNN* (1882).

M

magazines, magical. The first English magazine devoted strictly to conjuring was *Ellis Stanyon*'s *MAGIC* (1900–14, 1919–20). *THE MAGICIAN MONTHLY* (1904–39) was published by *Gamage's* and originally edited by *Will Goldston*, who issued his own *MAGAZINE OF MAGIC* (1914–17, 1919–22, 1930–4) after leaving Gamage's. Another magical dealer, Ornum (George Munro) issued *THE WIZARD* (1905–10) edited by *Selbit*, the title being changed to *THE MAGIC WAND* (1910–17, 1919–58) when Munro himself took over the editorship. This became one of the most notable of all magical journals, owned and edited for 30 years (1915–45) by *George Johnson*. Since the last war several interesting magical journals have appeared, among them *THE GEN* (1946–70) from the magic dealer *Harry Stanley*, *MAGIGRAM* (1966) from *Supreme Magic*, *THE PENTAGRAM* (1946–59) edited by *Warlock*, and *ABRACADABRA* (1946), the only weekly. *THE MAGIC CIRCULAR* (1906), organ of the *Magic Circle*, has the longest continuous run in the history of magical journals. American magazines include G. H. Little's *MAHATMA* (1895, 1898–1906), the earliest of all; *THE SPHINX* (1902–53), edited in its later years by *John Mulholland*; *HUGARD'S MAGIC MONTHLY* (1943–65); *THE PHOENIX* and *NEW PHOENIX* (1942–65); *Annemann*'s *JINX* (1934–41); and *GENII* (1936), issued by the Larsens (*Magic Castle*). *THE LINKING RING* (1923), organ of the *I.B.M.*, is one of the most substantial, each issue running to about 150 pages. *Illustrations 1, 94*. Numerous other magical magazines, some of them short-lived, have appeared in Britain, America and other countries.

magic. Force that achieves, or seems

The only paper in the British Empire devoted solely to the interests of Magicians, Jugglers, Hand Shadowists, Ventriloquists, Lightning Cartoonists and Speciality Entertainers.

VOL. II. No. 10.   Entered at Stationers Hall·   **JULY, 1902.**   Annual Subscription, by Post, 5s. 6d. $1.50 / Single Copy, by Post, - -   6½d. 15 cents

The Medium of Inkerman.

Facsimile reproduction from the poster of M. Robin, the celebrated French Conjurer, representing his stage setting at the Egyptian Hall, Piccadilly, London. Robin, a Hollander by birth, was born in the year 1805. He was lessee of the Egyptian Hall for a period of time from 1857. He died in Paris in the year 1874.

94. Front cover of the first British magic magazine. ('Magic', July 1902.)

to achieve, effects that are contrary to natural laws. One kind of magic is a serious attempt to accomplish this by carrying out mystical rituals. Another kind is an open pretence made simply for purposes of entertainment. 'Magic' is thus a somewhat ambiguous term, used sometimes in the one sense, sometimes in the other. The word derives from the magi, the 'wise men' of ancient Iran. *magician.*

'Magic'. First British *magazine* devoted solely to the interests of magicians and allied artists, founded, edited, and largely written by *Ellis Stanyon* (1900–14, 1919–20). Most issues included Explanatory Programmes, in which Stanyon gave detailed descriptions of the shows of contemporary magicians, with his own suggested explanations of their tricks – not always to their liking. *Illustration 94.*

Magic Castle. Building in the centre of Hollywood, opened as a luxurious magical club in 1963 by Bill and Milt Larsen. There are regular members (practising amateur or professional magicians) and associate members. Among other rooms the Castle includes a splendid dining-room, a magical library, and a magical museum. One or two 'resident' magicians are an extra attraction.

Magic Circle. Famous British magical society, based in London but with 1,500 members from all over the world. It was founded in 1905, with *Devant* and then *Nevil Maskelyne* as its earliest presidents. Its journal, *THE MAGIC CIRCULAR*, was started the following year. Members meet once a week at the headquarters, 84 Chenies Mews, near Gower Street; membership is open to men over 18 who have a real interest in the art of magic. Normally a member becomes first an Associate, and may in due course secure promotion to full membership, thence possibly to become an Associate of the Inner Magic Circle. Usually promotion is obtained by way of a specific examination performance. The highest distinction is to be a Member of the Inner Magic Circle, an honour normally awarded by invitation of the Council. The Circle's lending and reference libraries are notable; there is also a small theatre, and a museum of old conjuring apparatus, etc., some of which is on permanent display. The motto of the Circle is *Indocilis Privata Loqui* ('Not apt to disclose secrets') and its symbol the circular sign of the Zodiac, which appears even on the floor of the clubroom; *illustrations 95, 96.* Auction sales are held every six months, and a Magic Collectors' Day once a year; *illustration 66. magazines; societies.*

magic dealers. *dealers.*

'Magic Show, The'. *Henning, Douglas.*

magic square. A square of figures with each row (horizontal and vertical) adding up to the same total. The simplest form is:

$$
\begin{array}{ccc}
8 & 1 & 6 \\
3 & 5 & 7 \\
4 & 9 & 2
\end{array}
$$

The horizontal rows total 15 (e.g. $8+1+6$) and so do the vertical rows (e.g. $8+3+4$). Moreover, the diagonals do the same ($8+5+2$; $6+5+4$).

A simple four-column square is:

$$
\begin{array}{cccc}
7 & 12 & \mathbf{13} & 2 \\
\mathbf{14} & 1 & 8 & 11 \\
4 & \mathbf{15} & 10 & 5 \\
9 & 6 & 3 & \mathbf{16}
\end{array}
$$

Each row and diagonal total 34.

95. Magic Circle clubroom. The unusual stairs lead to the reference library and museum.

96. The Magic Circle theatre.

A spectator may be allowed to choose a number for the total. Suppose (for example) he chooses 45. Begin by deducting 34 from the chosen number ($45-34=11$). Then 11 is added to each of the bold numbers. If this is done it will be found that horizontals, verticals, and diagonals all add up to 45. Moreover, the four figures in each of the four corners also total 45. It is highly desirable either to memorize the basic square or to have it written somewhere where it can be *secretly* consulted. *mathematical magic.* See Simon, MATHEMATICAL MAGIC, pp.106–34. Royal Vale Heath, MATHEMAGIC, pp.87–98; Dexter, *FEATURE MAGIC FOR MENTALISTS*, pp.95–102; G. B. Anderson, *MAGIC DIGEST*, p.52.

magic wand. *wand.*

'Magic Wand, The'. Notable magical *magazine* owned and edited by George Munro (1910–14), then by *George Johnson* (1914–45), and finally by George Armstrong (1945–58). A monthly till 1921, then a quarterly.

magic words. Occult magicians have always been fascinated by the idea that 'words of power' can work marvels. Conjuring entertainers have naturally adopted the idea, and the utterance of a magic word is often used as the pretended key to a magical happening. Among popular words are *'Abracadabra'*, *'Hey Presto'*, and *'Hocus Pocus'*. An impressive favourite of *Hoffmann* was 'Aldiborontiphoscophornio' (actually a character in a popular eighteenth-century burlesque). *Dante* used 'Sim Sala Bim', nonsense words from an old Danish song. Other strange words will be found in most occult books or may be invented by the performer.

magical effects. Broadly speaking, there are about a dozen possible types of magical effect: (1) Production (e.g. *Aerial Treasury*); (2) Disappearance (e.g. *handkerchief vanish*); (3) Transposition (e.g. *Bottle and Glass Trick*); (4) Transformation (e.g. *Rice Bowls*); (5) Penetration (e.g. *Coin in Bottle*); (6) Invulnerability (e.g. *Bullet Catch*); (7) Restoration (e.g. *Decapitation Trick*); (8) Animation of the inanimate (e.g. *Rapping Hand*); (9) Defiance of gravity (e.g. *Floating Ball*); (10) Pseudo-psychic phenomena (e.g. *mentalism*); (11) Accelerated growth (e.g. *Mango Tree Trick*); (12) Overcoming of physical restrictions (e.g. *escapology*). Of course, a trick, still more a routine, may involve more than one of these effects.

magical history. *history of magic.*

magical societies. *Societies, Magical.*

magician. One who practises a form of *magic*, either an occult form or a form in which pretended mysteries are performed for entertainment. The term is thus ambiguous, but in this dictionary it is normally used only in the second sense. *conjurer*; *magicienne.*

magicienne. Female *magician*. *Magigals.*

Magigals. Organization of women magical performers in the U.S.A. and Canada, founded in 1938 by Frances Marshall.

magnetic pencil. Pencil that appears to adhere to the palm of the hand as a pin adheres to a magnet. A loop of thread, a pinhead in the pencil, or a finger of the other hand may be used; *illustration 97*. A ruler, wand, or pack of cards may also be 'magnetized'. See Severn, *MAGIC FROM YOUR POCKET*, pp.17–21.

'Mahatma'. First magazine devoted

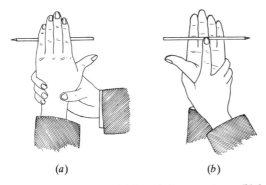

(a)   (b)

97. The magnetic pencil, (a) from in front or above, (b) from behind or below.

primarily to magic as an entertainment, published monthly in New York (1895, 1898–1906). Although an independent journal, it was for some time the official organ of the *Society of American Magicians.*

Malini, Max (Max K. Breit, 1873–1942). American magician born on the borders of Poland and Austria–Hungary, but taken to New York at an early age. As a private entertainer he was well-known to the élite and to magicians in almost every country, and was regarded as one of the most remarkable personalities the magical world has known. His story has been told by *Vernon*, edited by *Ganson* (1962).

Mango Tree Trick. Popular trick of the Indian *jadoo-wallahs*. A mango stone is placed in a mound of earth and covered with a small triangular tent. When this is removed it is seen that a small green shoot has sprung up. The process is repeated three or four times, the plant apparently growing larger each time. The last one may even have one or two fruits among the leaves. The secret is barefaced switching of plants beneath the ample tent cover.

manipulation. *sleight-of-hand* with

cards, coins, cigarettes, etc.

Marshall, Frances (Ireland). Very experienced American magicienne with a wide knowledge of magic, who began her magical career in the Chicago magic store of Laurie Ireland (1898–1954), whom she married. After his death she married *Jay Marshall.* Founder of the *Magigals*, and author of several books, including two lively conjuring gossip books, *YOU DON'T HAVE TO BE CRAZY* (1946) and a sequel, and (with Jay) a comprehensive book on making money from magic, *THE SUCCESS BOOK* (1973).

Marshall, Jay. Versatile American magician and ventriloquist, with the accent on comedy. His catchphrase, 'One of the better cheaper acts' is well-known in Britain as well as in the U.S.A., as is his left-hand glove puppet, Lefty. An expert on TV magic, author of *TV-MAGIC AND YOU* (1955). President of a leading American magical firm, Magic Inc., aided by his wife *Frances Marshall.* An enthusiastic magic collector.

Martin, John (*b*1882). Famous maker of magical apparatus, his pieces being greatly sought after. Born in Lithuania but settled in

London, and for some years worked exclusively for *De Biere*.

Maskelyne, Jasper (1902–73). Youngest grandson of *J. N. Maskelyne*, and the most capable performer of the family. For a time had charge of Maskelyne's Mysteries at *St George's Hall*, but later toured with his own act. A suave genial performer, he was a loss to magic when he gave up to farm in Kenya.

Maskelyne, John Nevil (1839–1917). One of the great names in magic. His magical career began in 1865 when he discovered the *Davenport Brothers* cheating and later, with *George Cooke*, reproduced their feats. Soon after this he gave up his work as watchmaker and became a professional conjurer. In 1873 he took a room in the *Egyptian Hall*, where he remained for 30 years, making it 'England's Home of Mystery'. In 1905 he transferred to *St George's Hall*. Maskelyne was greater as inventor and maker of magical apparatus than as performer, though he was a superb plate-spinner. Among his inventions were the *Box Trick*, a brilliant *Floating Lady*, and a number of remarkable automata, including *Psycho*. He became involved in litigation over challenges in connection with the Box Trick and with a spiritualist, Archdeacon Colley. Maskelyne lost both cases, though the publicity may have been useful to the Home of Mystery. His writings include *MODERN SPIRITUALISM* (1875) and *SHARPS AND FLATS* (1894), exposures respectively of spiritualism and gambling. His two sons, *Nevil* and Archie (E.A.), and his three grandsons, all played a part in Maskelyne's Home of Mystery (1873–1933). *Illustrations 6, 98. levitation.*

Maskelyne, Nevil (1863–1924). Elder son of *J.N.M.* and for many years manager of the Maskelyne Home of Mystery. Author of the theoretical part of *OUR MAGIC* (1911). His sons Clive (1895–1927), Noel (1898–1976), and *Jasper* (1902–1973) all performed at *St George's Hall*. *Magic Circle.*

Maskelyne and Cooke. *Maskelyne, J. N.; Cooke; Egyptian Hall.*

Maskelyne and Devant. *Maskelyne, J. N.; Devant; St George's Hall.*

matchboxes, rattling. *rattle bars.*

mathematical magic. A good many tricks are based on mathematical principles. They include feats involving apparent lightning calculation, *predictions*, *magic squares*, the *Knight's Tour*, tricks with dates and calendars, and various tricks with dice, dominoes, and playing-cards. The figure 9 plays an important part in many mathematical tricks. For example, if the figures 1 to 9 (excluding 8) are multiplied by a chosen figure (e.g. 5) and that result by 9, the result will be a row of the chosen figures (e.g. 555,555,555). Useful books include William Simon, *MATHEMATICAL MAGIC* (1964); Gardner, *MATHEMATICS, MAGIC, AND MYSTERY* (1956).

Matter through Matter. *penetration.*

McComb, William. Clever and experienced professional conjurer from Northern Ireland, noted for his humour and for the effective presentation of simple effects such as *Coin in Bottle*, and Gipsy Thread. Intended originally for the medical profession, he was a student at Queen's University, Belfast. Author of *THE FIRST BOOK OF WILLIAM* (1947) and *McCOMB'S MAGIC* (1972).

medium. In *mentalism* an *assistant* who acts the part of a receiver of telepathic messages from the performer or from another assistant. The term derives from spiritualism, the medium here acting as an agent through whom the spirits of the dead supposedly communicate.

98. 'J. N. Maskelyne' floating at the Egyptian Hall.

memorization. One form of *mentalism*, involving apparently remarkable memorizing ability. The commonest feat, often known as the *Giant Memory*, is performed by the use of a mnemonic, which enables a long list of numbered objects to be precisely remembered without difficulty. Another form of mnemonic is to associate a letter with each primary number. For example, 1=*l* (one stroke), 2=n (two strokes), 3=m (three strokes), 4=r, 5=f/v, 6=b, 7=t, 8=sh, 9=g. The mnemonic may be used in various ways. Thus a long number may be remembered through the initial letters (excluding vowels) of words in a sentence (e.g. 32142563497 – My New Librarian Reads No Fiction But Mysteries Or Ghost Tales).

Other secret aids may be involved. For instance, the memorizing of a long sequence of playing-cards may be simulated by the use of a *prearranged* pack. See Fred Barlow, *MENTAL PRODIGIES*, pp.174–82, 194; Hugard, *ENCYCLOPEDIA OF CARD TRICKS*, pp.428–31; Scarne, *SCARNE'S MAGIC TRICKS*, pp.228–9.

Mene-Tekel pack. Pack of playing-cards consisting of 26 *short cards* duplicating 26 ordinary cards. They are arranged with each short card immediately above its duplicate. They can be *riffled* to show all cards apparently different, but a spectator who inserts his finger during the riffle will inevitably take a short card. If the cards are cut here the duplicate of his card will be brought to the top of the pack, where it can be discovered in various ways. (See Hugard, *ENCYCLOPEDIA OF CARD TRICKS*, pp.284–9.) The name Mene-Tekel is hardly appropriate, these being two of the words written on the wall at Belshazzar's feast and grimly interpreted by Daniel (*DANIEL*, v). *Robert-Houdin* used them, also curiously, for *Cards Across*.

mentalism. Name given by conjurers to any form of magic which involves the mind rather than the hand or mechanical apparatus. Mentalism includes *divination, thought-reading, prediction, memorization, lie detection, muscle-reading, sightless vision, book tests*. Such mental feats fall broadly into two groups: (1) those performed with a partner or *medium*; (2) those performed by the performer working alone. Tricks under (1) are generally performed by some kind of code. Those under (2) may involve *billet-reading* or the *one-ahead system*. Opinions may differ on how far a mentalist is justified in pretending to possess genuine psychic powers, but the danger of charlatanry should certainly be avoided by making clear that the intention of the performance is simply entertainment. Among performers who have specialized in mentalism are *Heller*, the *Zancigs, Dunninger*, the *Piddingtons, Berglas, Fogel, Kreskin, Koran, Nelson, Annemann, Warlock*. Many books are available: e.g. Lamb, *YOUR BOOK OF MENTAL MAGIC* (1973); Adair, *MENTAL MAGIC* (1961); Ganson, *MAGIC OF THE MIND* (1972); Corinda, *13 STEPS TO MENTALISM* (1958) – a comprehensive guide. Many general conjuring books contain a section on mental magic.

Merlin. Famous wizard of King Arthur's legendary court, tales of whom were first told by twelfth-century Geoffrey of Monmouth and later in Malory's *MORTE D'ARTHUR* (c.1470).

Metamorphosis. *Substitution Trunk.*

Metempsychosis. Popular nine-teenth-century illusion developed by *Pepper*, in which a person might appear to change visibly into someone else, or one object into another. It was worked on the *mirror principle*, a reflection taking the place of the original as a large mirror was pushed slowly forward; *Illustration 99*. See Lamb, *VICTORIAN MAGIC*, pp.47–50, *PEGASUS BOOK OF MAGICIANS*, pp.29–30; Dexter, *THIS IS MAGIC*, pp.40–2; Pepper, *The True History of The Ghost.*

Mexican turnover. Method of secretly changing a playing-card that is face-down on the table (say a King) with one in the performer's hand (an indifferent card). An edge of the latter is slipped under the King and begins to turn it over. But when the two cards are roughly upright the performer's fingers slip imperceptibly from the indifferent card to the King; *illustration 100*. Thus the former is left face-up on the table (as if it had just been turned over) while the King is removed. The sleight is sometimes used in the *Three-card Trick* if a spectator happens to pick the right card.

M.I.M.C. Member of the Inner Magic Circle, an advanced qualification with which about one tenth of the members are honoured. *Magic Circle.*

mind-reading. *mentalism.*

mirror glass. Glass tumbler divided lengthwise into two compartments by a mirror (sometimes removable) running from near the top to the bottom. With a handkerchief (say) in the rear compartment the tumbler should appear empty to the audience, but secretly turned round (under cover) the glass will reveal the handkerchief. Conversely, it can

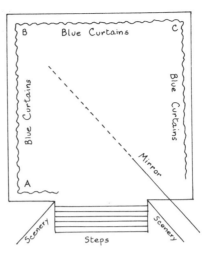

99. Metempsychosis.

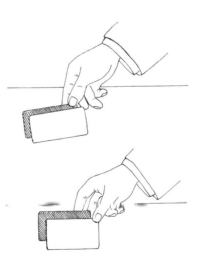

100. Mexican turnover. Performer's fingers and thumb slide from the back (shaded) card to the front one.

103

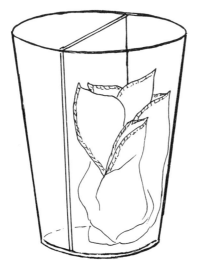

101. Mirror glass.

be used to vanish an article. Unfortunately, many mirror glasses look suspicious; they should be used with caution. *Illustration 101*.

mirror principle. Two mirrors placed beneath a three-legged table in the form of a V, with the join nearest the audience, will reflect what is at the side. If the side reflection resembles what is at the back of the stage the audience will appear to have a clear view under the table, though a person or object is in fact hidden behind the mirrors. This principle has often been used in stage illusions in various ways, both under tables (e.g. *Sphinx*) and inside cabinets. *Proteus Cabinet*; *Sword Cabinet*.

misdirection. The basic essential of all good conjuring; the subtle art of leading audiences to misinterpret what they see. This should not be confused with *distraction*, which tries to prevent the audience from seeing what is happening by drawing attention away from it. Misdirection, properly applied, is constantly in operation throughout a competent magician's routine, and is based not on distracting actions but on natural movements. The performer does what appears to be the natural thing, but he does it in a way and for a reason that the audience does not realize. A very simple instance. The conjurer wishes to slip into his pocket an object (concealed in his left hand) which the spectators believe to be held in his right hand. If he 'clumsily' knocks something off his table while his left hand steals surreptitiously to his pocket, that is *distraction*. But if he casually brings a handkerchief from his left pocket to wrap up the object supposedly in his right hand, that is *misdirection*, the natural movement of bringing out a handkerchief disguising the dropping of the object in the pocket. A series of distractions would spoil a performance, whereas a series of misdirections, by their naturalness, leave the audience pleasantly deceived.

Miser's Dream. *Aerial Treasury*.

M.M.C. Member of the *Magic Circle*.

'Modern Magic'. *Hoffmann*.

monte. Spanish–American card gambling game, played with 45 cards. Three-card monte is a Mexican version of the *three-card trick*.

Morritt, Charles (1861–1936). Skilful English conjurer and magical inventor who preceded *Devant* at the *Egyptian Hall* under *Maskelyne*. His most famous tricks were probably the Disappearing Donkey and an illusion called 'Oh!' in which a man vanished while being held by members of the audience. An effective thought-reading act with his sister was also included in his act during his long 50-year career, which began in 1878.

move. Secret manoeuvre (which may or may not be a *sleight*) necessary for the performance of a trick.

Mulholland, John (1898–1970). American magician, at one time a school teacher. Editor of *THE SPHINX* for over 20 years, consultant on conjuring to several reference book publishers, and a leading authority on every aspect of magic. Author of *QUICKER THAN THE EYE* (1928), *STORY OF MAGIC* (1935), *BOOK OF MAGIC* (1963), and other important contributions to magical literature.

Multiplying Billiard Balls. *Billiard Balls*.

Multiplying Bottles. *Bottle and Glass Trick*.

Murray (Leo Murray Carrington-Walters). Famous Australian magician and *escapologist* (he coined the word), who for a short while was assistant to *Le Roy*. He has appeared in 87 different countries, often under the title, 'King of Entertainers, Entertainer of Kings'. After World War II he created a substantial magic show but was forced by illness in 1954 to retire to Blackpool, where he keeps a novelty and magic store.

muscle reading. Type of *mind-reading* with physical contact between performer and volunteer assistant. After an object has been hidden the volunteer takes the hand of the sometimes blindfolded performer, concentrates on the object, and unwittingly guides him by unconsciously exercising slight pressure when he moves in the wrong direction. Many elaborations have been worked out. Notable muscle-readers have been *Bishop*, Randall Brown, Stuart Cumberland, Alfred Capper, and *George Kreskin*.

Mutus, Dedit . . . Old method of card location. Twenty cards are placed on the table face down in pairs, and one or more pairs are chosen and noted by spectators. The performer then gathers up the pairs in any order and throws them down again apparently at random but really in a set pattern represented by the Latin words:

M	U	T	U	S
D	E	D	I	T
N	O	M	E	N
C	O	C	I	S

Thus the first pair to be thrown down are placed in the M positions, the second pair in the U positions, and so on. If a spectator now indicates in which row(s) his cards are, the performer can pick out the cards. The trick has been described in many books: e.g. Hoffmann, *MODERN MAGIC*, pp.54–5; Scarne, *SCARNE ON CARD TRICKS*, pp.101–3; Lamb, *TABLE TRICKS*, pp.28–30; Harbin, *HOW TO BE A WIZARD*, pp.61–5.

N

nail-writer. Gimmick that fits on the thumbnail or fingernail for secretly writing a prediction or other example of *mentalism. thumbwriter. Illustration 144.*

Nap, Conjurer's. Five cards each are given to five people as in the game of Nap (Napoleon). Each person is asked to choose mentally a card from his hand, after which the cards are collected and dealt again in five heaps. The performer takes each heap in turn; when anyone says he sees his card, the performer at once names it. Assuming that the hands as collected were placed one above the other, when the cards are re-dealt the first in each heap must be from the original hand of spectator 5 (last hand to be collected), the next card in each heap from the original hand of spectator 4, and so on. It is desirable for some mystic rite to be performed with the cards before the re-deal, as an excuse for collecting them up.

Needle Trick. Sensational trick in which the performer puts a bundle of needles into his mouth, followed by some thread. After pretending to swallow them he draws from his mouth a long line of threaded needles, sometimes stretching right across the stage. The secret is a *switch* of needle bundles. The trick was a favourite of *Houdini.* See Anderson, *MAGIC DIGEST*, pp.201–3. The trick is also performed with razor blades.

Nelson, Robert. American performer, dealer, and author concerned almost exclusively with *mentalism* in its various aspects. A prolific writer (perhaps too prolific and repetitive), with the (misnamed) *ENCYCLOPEDIA OF MENTALISM* (1944) his chief work.

nest of boxes. Series of boxes each of which (except the biggest) fits inside one slightly larger. A coin, ring, or watch is vanished, and is ultimately found inside the smallest box. Each box has to be separately opened before the next can be removed, though all the lids can be closed together in a single movement. The number and design of the boxes varies considerably. Some types are self-locking, with hinged lids; others may be closed with rubber bands. The lids are propped open in some way until the article (usually borrowed) can be secretly inserted. Small nests may be in the performer's pocket, larger ones hidden behind some bulkier apparatus on the table until needed. A nest of zip-fastening purses is a recent development.

nicking. Marking a playing-card with the thumbnail, leaving an indentation, so that the card can be recognized by touch or sight.

Nicola, The Great (William Mozart Nicol, 1880–1946). Popular illusionist, reputed to be the highest paid of all American magicians. He toured America and the East extensively with his elaborate show, which included a Vanishing Elephant, but his name was little known in Britain.

Nikola system. Card *set-up* invented by Louis Nikola (William Smith), a clever conjurer who performed many times at *St George's Hall* in the first two decades of this century. The set-up can withstand fairly thorough investigation without arousing suspicion (though every fourth card is a heart), but the almost random arrangement of the cards has to be memorized. Although a mnemonic is employed (*memorization*) a good deal of hard mental work is involved. Most beginners, at any rate, may feel that they can achieve adequate results by a set-up more easily remembered. The Nikola system is described in Hugard, *ENCYCLOPEDIA OF CARD TRICKS*, pp.426–45.

Nixon, David (1919–78). Famous English magician who first became a professional entertainer with the Fol de Rols concert party, after which he appeared at the *Windmill Theatre*. His first TV performance was in 1950, since when he became a well-known TV personality, with several magic shows to his credit. Magic's image has been well served by his easy manner, pleasant humour, and good showmanship, admirably supported by the magical ingenuity of *Ali Bongo*, closely associated with most of Nixon's TV shows; *illustration 102*.

Nose Trick. Old Elizabethan trick described by *Scot*, the basis of the *Pillars of Solomon*, and performed in the same way. The apparatus, known as a bridle, was placed over somebody's nose, through which the

102. Ali Bongo threatening a captive balloon.

107

cord appeared to pass. Often a pretence was first made of boring a hole through the nose. *Illustration 103.*

Nudist pack. Cards which appear to be blank on both sides. Subsequently faces and then backs are shown to be mysteriously printed on the cards. Each blank card is in fact two cards *roughed* together, one having a face on the inner surface, the other a back. Obtainable from dealers.

103. Elizabethan Nose Trick.

O

Obedient Ball. Old trick in which a wooden ball threaded on a cord stops in its descent at the word of command. The cord does not run straight through the ball, the hole being slightly bent; *illustration 104.*

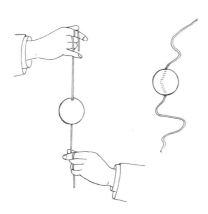

104. The Obedient Ball.

By tightening the cord, the performer can check the ball's downward movement. Later developments have allowed the ball to rise as well as fall, either through a pulley system inserted within the ball or by use of a thread. *Devant* used a large ball in a stage trick: it ran up or down a long plank according to orders (e.g. 'Go slowly', 'Come through this ring', etc.). See Devant, SECRETS OF MY MAGIC, pp.79–81; Hoffmann, MODERN MAGIC, pp.301–3, MORE MAGIC, pp.279–84.

Odds and Evens. Arrangement of playing-cards, all of odd value being put in one half, all of even value in the other (Q even; J, K, odd). Each half may be given to a different spectator to shuffle and to select a card. If the halves are secretly transposed before the selected cards are returned, one odd card will be among the evens and vice versa, and thus easily discoverable by the performer.

Okito (Theodore Bamberg, 1875–1963). Descendant of a long line of Dutch magicians (*Bambergs*). He toured widely, appearing many times in Britain, but settled in the U.S.A. His foreign costume was originally Japanese and his stage-name an anagram of Tokio, but later he preferred the colourful Chinese robes and performed as a Chinaman. At one period he was a magic dealer in New York, and he also joined the *Thurston* show for a short while. His own act was clever and attractive, though sometimes marred by excessive use of livestock. Perhaps his best and most effective trick was the *Floating Ball*. Some of his tricks are described in his *QUALITY MAGIC* (1921) and the partly autobiographical *OKITO ON MAGIC* (1952). See also Albo, Lewis, and Bamberg, *ORIENTAL MAGIC OF THE BAMBERGS* (1973); H. R. Evans, *ADVENTURES IN MAGIC* (1927).

Okito Coin Box. Small circular metal box for vanishing coins. The lid fits over either end, and by secretly

105. Okito Coin Box.

transferring it from top to bottom of the box the performer can secure possession of the coin within; *illustration 105*. Some skill is required to perform the move convincingly.

one-ahead system. Term for a familiar method of *divination*. Briefly, the performer 'divines' three or more cards or *billets* by slyly being one step ahead each time. Thus with three cards face down on the table, having secretly found out that Card 3 (say) is a Queen, he gives *this* name to Card 1, which (looking at it as if to verify his statement) he finds is (say) a 10. He therefore names Card 2 as 'Ten', looks and finds it to be an Ace, and proceeds to name Card 3 as 'Ace'. He has apparently named each of the three cards before looking at them, and now holds them in his hand as 'proof' that his divinations were correct. An essential of the system is, of course, a pre-knowledge of *one* item, gained usually by previous *glimpsing* or by secretly substituting a billet of his own for one of the others. See Scarne, *SCARNE'S MAGIC TRICKS*, pp.150–1; Elliott, *MAGIC AS A HOBBY*, pp.178–82.

one-man mentalism. Mind-reading act or trick without a partner or *medium*. Thought-reading *with* such a partner is *two-person telepathy*. *one-ahead system*; *billet reading*.

one-way cards. Cards whose backs show either a picture or a pattern which differs according to which way up the card is held. If all the cards are the same way up to start with, and the pack is turned round before a selected card is replaced, the performer can easily pick it out with the cards face down. The principle needs to be used with subtlety; it is the basis of a number of ingenious tricks. *one-way faces*; *reversed* *cards*. See Hugard, ENCYCLOPEDIA OF CARD TRICKS, pp.154–85.

one-way faces. Even where playing-cards have symmetrical backs, 22 of them can be made into *one-way* cards when they are face-up: A, 3, 5, 6, 7, 8, 9 of clubs, hearts, and spades, plus 7 of diamonds. Cards of the first three suits can be so arranged that there are more pips pointing down than up, while 7D can be put the same way up as 7H. Arranged thus they become one-way cards; *illustration 106.*

ably. A trick involving a number of preliminaries, such as borrowing or examining articles, or having cards chosen, is generally a *bad* opener.

optical illusion. Deception caused by misleading the eye, as with tricks involving the *mirror principle* or *black art*. Puzzles connected with size and shape may also come into this category; *illustrations 107, 108.* See Brewster, LETTERS ON NATURAL MAGIC, Letters 2–6.

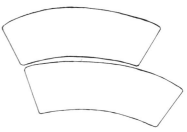

107. Optical illusion. Which boomerang is the larger?

106. Cards with one-way faces. Clubs, spades, and hearts have most pips pointing down. 7D is same way up as 7H.

108. Optical illusion. Which line is the longer?

opening trick. Although it is impossible to lay down rules (performers and circumstances differ), a sound general principle is to begin a performance with a trick which does not take too long and which enables the performer to show himself favour-

ordinary. Applied to any article that is not *faked*. The performer, however, should beware of describing an article as 'ordinary' in his patter. If an article *looks* ordinary the audience will usually assume that it is, unless told otherwise.

organizations, magical. *societies, magical.*

110

Origami. Japanese word for paper folding, originally a Japanese art.

'Our Magic'. Famous conjuring book by *Maskelyne* (Nevil) and *Devant* (1911). The first two sections, by Maskelyne, deal at length with interesting theories and precepts ('The Art in Magic', 'The Theory of Magic'). The third gives detailed, illustrated descriptions of how 12 of Devant's *St George's Hall* tricks were performed. The first part of the book is inclined to be verbose, but Devant's very precise explanations and instructions are illuminating and invaluable.

out. Way out of a dilemma; a subterfuge which can be adopted to avoid complete failure when something goes wrong with a trick.

Out of This World. Brilliant card trick in which a spectator is invited to deal the cards into two heaps, putting each card into whichever heap he pleases – only to find that he has dealt all the reds in one heap and all the blacks in the other. Invented by Paul Curry, who explains it in *MAGICIAN'S MAGIC* (1965).

overhand shuffle. Perhaps the commonest form of card shuffle. The pack is held in the left hand. The right hand lifts off most of the lower (right) part of the pack and drops it in a series of very small packets on the other (left) side of the remaining cards. Each packet falls to the left of the preceding packet.

P

pack. Complete set of 52 playing-cards plus 2 Jokers. *deck*.

packet. Group of cards cut or dealt from the pack. Also heap, pile.

paddle move. Simple sleight widely used in many forms, basically with a 'paddle', a kind of tiny cricket bat; *illustration 109*. The performer first shows both sides apparently blank. Then a coloured mark suddenly appears on both sides. Finally there is a mark on one side but not on the other, at which point the paddle can be examined if desired. The secret move is that as the performer turns his hand to (apparently) show the

109. Typical paddle.

other side of the paddle he also gives the handle a slight twist in his fingers, thus causing the same side of the paddle to be shown twice. He can choose whether to show both sides apparently blank or apparently marked. A great many variations are possible, both with a paddle and with other articles, such as knives and penknives. See Baron, *CLOSE-UP MAGIC FOR BEGINNERS*, pp.91–100; Elliott, *CLASSIC SECRETS OF MAGIC*, pp.46–50.

Page, Patrick. Accomplished Scottish close-up conjurer, for a time manager of Davenports. Author of useful little books on card, coin, handkerchief, and paper magic, and of *THE BIG BOOK OF MAGIC* (1976).

'Palingenesia'. Fanciful name for one of *Lynn*'s most famous illusions. An assistant was fastened to a door, after which his limbs and head were apparently hacked off in turn. He was of course put together again later, and the sensational trick was presented with Dr Lynn's customary humour. See Lamb, *VICTORIAN MAGIC*, pp.93–4.

palm. To conceal an article within the hand in an unobtrusive way. A playing-card is held within the whole hand, with fingers closed and slightly curved. A pack is sometimes handed (palm down) to a spectator with the hand that holds a palmed card. A coin is either *finger-palmed*, *thumb-palmed*, or retained by pressure in the fleshy part of the palm. Other articles of reasonable size may be similarly palmed. The essential thing is that the hand should be held naturally, with the back of the hand towards the audience. *back-palm*; *pass*(2).

palming coin. One specially made of light metal with a milled edge, and therefore easy to palm.

Parasol, Mutilated. *Sunshade Trick*.

parlour tricks. Simple conjuring tricks and puzzles suitable for the amusement of a small gathering of friends. *drawing-room magic*.

pass (1). Basic card sleight by which the lower half of the pack is secretly made to become the upper half, a common use of the sleight being to bring a selected card to the top of the pack. The card is placed by the spectator on the lower half (in the performer's left hand), and as the top half is brought over it the left little finger slips between the two halves; *illustration 110*. The upper half is

110. The pass: little finger slipped between two halves.

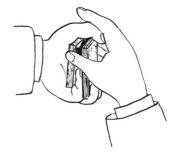

111. The pass: lower half about to be levered upward.

tilted by the little finger (below) and other fingers (above) of the left hand, while the right hand levers the lower half upwards against the left thumb; *illustration 111*. The two halves just clear each other and then change places, the former upper half now being the lower, and vice versa. To accomplish the sleight quickly and indetectably needs a great deal of practice and some skilful *misdirection*. See Gibson, *COMPLETE ILLUSTRATED BOOK OF CARD MAGIC*, pp.64–9; Baron, *CARD TRICKS FOR BEGINNERS*, pp.25–33. Hugard and Braue, *ROYAL ROAD TO CARD MAGIC*, pp.165–8.

pass (2). To make the pass with any other article than a card is to simulate transferring it from one hand to the other while really retaining it palmed in the original hand. There are various methods, the easiest being the *French Drop*. *thimble manipulation*.

pass (3). Gesture of the hands, usually accompanied by magic words,. ostensibly in order to accomplish a magical result.

Passe-Passe Trick. *Bottle and Glass Trick*. *Passe-passe* is French for 'sleight-of-hand'.

pasteboard. *playing-card*.

patter. Conjurer's conversation while performing. This affects the whole tone of the performance; it should appear natural and spontaneous, even though it may have been learnt to some extent by heart. It should be consistent in style, and preferably light-hearted, while avoiding the laboured facetiousness of the patter which many older books (e.g. *Goldston*'s) give for each trick. Patter should reflect the personality of the individual performer, unless he is deliberately acting a special part (e.g. costermonger, country bump-

kin). Tastes and talents vary, but with any performer the timing and main points of the patter should be known by heart, even if the actual words are allowed to come spontaneously.

peek. Glance secretly (usually at a playing-card). *glimpse*.

pencil and paper tricks. Tricks involving some form of writing by performer and/or spectator; often *mathematical tricks*, *optical puzzles*, tricks with words or diagrams, and feats of *mentalism*. Many books on mentalism include pencil and paper tricks. See also Gardner, *MATHEMATICS, MAGIC, AND MYSTERY*, pp.129–74; Lamb, *PENCIL AND PAPER TRICKS* (U.S.A.).

pencil reading. The art of seeing from the movements of a spectator's pencil and hand just what number (or even word) he is writing. Though advocated by some *mentalists*, such reading has limited value in conjuring performances. The first thing many people will expect a performer to do is to try and glimpse what they are writing, and as a rule he must show clearly (e.g. by turning his back) that he is *not* doing so.

penetration. The passing of one solid object through another without damaging either. It takes many forms, from simple parlour tricks (e.g. a finger pushed through a hat) to elaborate stage illusions (e.g. *Walking through a Brick Wall*). Several standard tricks involve penetration, either as part of an effect (e.g. *Card through Handkerchief*) or as the main effect, sometimes known as Matter through Matter. Objects are often passed through a sheet of glass or a borrowed handkerchief. The latter may be pinned to a picture frame; under cover of a paper bag solid articles

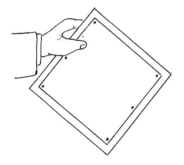

112. Penetration: handkerchief pinned to frame.

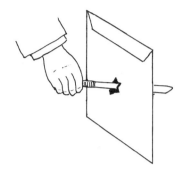

114. Knife apparently penetrates handkerchief.

113. Frame inserted in paper bag.

115. Top of frame drops down, allowing handkerchief (shaded) to be secretly moved aside.

such as pencils, knives, pipes, and walking-sticks are pushed straight through. The top section of the frame is secretly hinged, dropping down under cover of the paper bag and taking the handkerchief with it; *illustrations 112–15*.

pentagram. Five-sided figure of great magical significance; *illustration 116*. A useful symbol to bear in mind when performing a trick involving the number 5 (e.g. with 5 heaps of cards, or with a number to

116. Pentagram; the two points are directed downward, necessary in white Magic.

114

be multiplied by 5). *PENTAGRAM* (1946–59) was the title of a monthly magical journal, edited by *Warlock*, devoted particularly to *mentalism*; it has been succeeded by *NEW PENTAGRAM* (1969), also edited by Warlock, and published by Supreme Magic Co. *magazines, magical.*

Pepper, John Henry (1821–1900). Director of the Royal Polytechnic Institute, London, and lecturer on popular science, usually known as Professor Pepper. Notable for his presentation of the *Ghost Trick*, first seen at the Polytechnic and commonly known as Pepper's Ghost; *illustration 74.* He wrote several popular scientific books: e.g. *THE BOY'S PLAYBOOK OF SCIENCE* (1860); *THE BOY'S PLAYBOOK OF METALS* (1861). Despite their titles, they are more serious than playful.

Peters, Howard. Has been called the British version of Houdini. He has travelled widely, escaping from handcuffs, strait-jackets, icy rivers, the *Water Torture Cell*, etc.; he also engages in fire-eating. In October 1977 he took the part of Houdini as escapist in a curious Dutch opera produced in Amsterdam.

phantom tube. Long tube used for magical productions of silks, coils, etc. Within the main tube there is an inner tube tapering at one end to a smaller circumference, and attached at the other end to the main tube. Looked at from this latter end the tube appears empty, but the *load* is in fact packed between the two tubes; *illustration 117.* Also known as ghost tube.

Phillippe (Jacques Talon, 1802–78). French magician who began as a confectioner in France and Britain but later switched to conjuring. He was influenced by some Chinese conjurers seen in Ireland, and he always presented half of his act in Chinese costume, featuring the production of several bowls of goldfish – an effect widely copied by other magicians.

Piddingtons, The. Sydney Piddington and his wife, Lesley, both Australians, created quite a furore in Britain with their supposed telepathy on radio, 1949–50, but retired early from show business. Many laymen believed strongly that the Piddingtons had genuine telepathic powers. The performers themselves discreetly said, 'We leave it to you'.

pile. *packet* or *heap* of playing-cards.

Pillars of Solomon. Rather pretentious name for a simple little trick popular in Victorian times and still seen, based on the old Elizabethan *Nose Trick.* Two small ornamented pieces of stick are hinged at the bottom and apparently joined at the top by a length of string running loosely through them from side to side. A knife is passed between them so as to cut the string, the severed ends of which are visible. Yet when the sticks are placed together again the string runs through as freely as before. The secret is that the string

117. Phantom tube. Space labelled A is loaded.

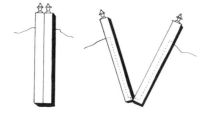

118. Pillars of Solomon.

really runs down each stick and across at the hinged bottom; *illustration 118*. The severed ends are dummies. *Chinese Sticks*.

Pinetti, Guiseppe (c.1750–1800). Probably the leading conjurer of the eighteenth century, a fashionable Italian performer who entertained royalty in several countries. Despite the efforts of a French amateur, Henri Decremps, to denigrate him in a series of expository books (useful and interesting in themselves), he was apparently successful almost everywhere, especially in France and Russia. Two of his most notable tricks seem to have been a second sight act with his wife, and (strangely) the removal of a man's shirt without disturbing his coat.

pistol, conjurer's. Pocket pistol with a funnel fixed to the barrel for the reception of an article such as a handkerchief or watch. On being fired towards (say) a *nest of boxes* the article vanishes and is found within the boxes. A fairly shallow cap fits into the mouth of the funnel, enabling the article to be palmed off; *illustration 119*. The pistol fires either a blank charge or something even more harmless. *Devant* avoided even this, removing the funnel and simply blowing through it in order to vanish the article. Comic pistols are supplied by some dealers; when fired these release a small banner bearing the word 'Bang!'; *illustration 120*.

plant. *confederate*. Used also of something given to a confederate to offer to the performer as a borrowed article.

plug-box. Apparatus for vanishing a coin, which is dropped into a tubular brass container about 7 cm (3 in) long, closed by the insertion of a solid-looking brass plug of the same length. This is really faked and allows the coin to fall into the performer's hand.

pochettes. Small pockets at the back of the trouser-legs, for *stealing* or *secreting* coins or similar articles.

pocket tricks. Literally tricks which can be carried in a jacket or trouser pocket, and hence any tricks requiring only small, simple apparatus, such as coins, matchboxes, penknives, string, etc. If this is faked an

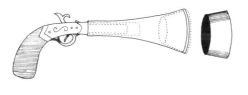

119. Conjurer's pistol, with cap.

120. 'Bang' pistol.

unfaked duplicate should be available for inspection.

Pollock, Channing. Suave and elegant American magician who made a great impression in the 1950s with his smooth manipulative act. Though skilful with balls, coins, and cards, he unfortunately chose to specialize in *dove* productions, which have since been sadly overdone. He retired early from magic and became a film actor.

Potter Index. A full index of tricks and the books and journals in which they are described, a mammoth undertaking made by Jack Potter, spread over many years. Now published as *THE MASTER INDEX TO MAGIC IN PRINT* (1967–75) – expensive but valuable.

practice. Performance of a sleight or trick in private so that it can be accomplished in public without the least fumbling or hesitation. Certain sleights (e.g. *thumb palm*) can be practised while sitting or walking, with the hand in a pocket; others are best practised before a mirror. Some conjurers distinguish between *practice* (of sleights) and *rehearsal* (of complete tricks). By whichever name, both are vitally important. Even a so-called *self-working trick* needs to be privately tried out again and again until the best way of presenting it becomes second nature.

prearrangement. Arrangement of cards in a special order. The best-known systems are the *Eight Kings* and the *Si Stebbins*, both of which are easy to remember. The *Nikola* system involves considerable memorizing. A prearranged pack can be cut repeatedly without altering the effective order of the cards. The performer has only to *glimpse* the bottom card to know the order

of the rest. The identity of a chosen card can be known by glimpsing the card above. See Hugard, *ENCYCLOPEDIA OF CARD TRICKS*, pp.211–71; Hay, *AMATEUR MAGICIAN'S HANDBOOK*, pp.218–19.

precognition. Supposed awareness of an event before it has happened, simulated by conjurers in making *predictions*.

prediction. Type of *mentalism* in which the performer correctly forecasts (for example) what card will be chosen, or the total of a sum as yet unknown, or a newspaper headline for a day in the future. There are many ways of performing such feats, some involving *forcing*, some the secret substitution of the correct answer for a blank *billet*, some the use of a nail-writer.

preparation. Secret arrangements required for a trick before a performance, such as the placing of threads for *Rising Cards* or *Floating Ball*, or the *prearrangement* of a pack of cards.

prestidigitation. Literally quickness of the fingers. The word has become applicable to any form of conjuring, not merely *sleight-of-hand*, but is either slightly pompous or slightly humorous.

prestidigitator. *conjurer. prestidigitation.*

Price, Harry (1881–1948). Remarkable personality in the magic world, a well-known investigator and writer concerning psychic matters, with a fair knowledge of conjuring. His splendid magical library, containing many rare occult and conjuring books, was presented to the University of London (1936), where it has been admirably cared for, and can be consulted by serious students on special application. Despite his undoubted abilities Price was an ambiguous personality, sometimes evasive (as in controversy with the *Magic Circle*) and lacking in integrity (as in his Borley Rectory adventures). None the less, some of his many books are full of interest (e.g. *SEARCH FOR TRUTH*, 1942; *50 YEARS OF PSYCHICAL RESEARCH*, 1939). See Dingwall, Goldney, and Hall, *THE HAUNTING OF BORLEY RECTORY* (1955) and Trevor H. Hall, *Search for Harry Price* (1978).

produce. Make a *production*.

production. Act of bringing articles into view from a container (e.g. hat, box, tube) that has previously been shown empty, or from an apparently empty hand. *Aerial Treasury*; *ghost tube*; *hat productions*; *Inexhaustible box*.

production box. *Inexhaustible box*.

profondes. Large pockets in the tails of an evening suit for receiving articles to be *ditched*.

props. *Apparatus* or other equipment required by a conjurer for a performance. Derived from theatrical slang for stage properties.

Protean act. *quick-change* magic. *Proteus cabinet*.

Proteus cabinet. Wooden cabinet invented by *Pepper and Tobin* for mysterious disappearances and transformations of people; in Greek legend Proteus was gifted with the power of assuming different identities. Although the cabinet was kept under close and continuous observation by spectators, an assistant who entered it was changed almost instantly into somebody quite different, after which the original assistant would reappear, and the spectators on the stage were invited to examine the cabinet inside and out. It was based on the *mirror principle*, two mirrors being opened out

121. Proteus cabinet, with mirrors opened to centre.

to form a V (the join being hidden by a central pillar) behind which one or more persons could be concealed; *illustration 121*. After use the mirrors could be folded back against the sides of the cabinet, which they exactly resembled. *sword cabinet*.

Psycho. Automaton developed by *J. N. Maskelyne* in 1875 from a prototype suggested by J. A. Clarke. It took the form of an Indian figure, two feet high, isolated from the stage by a clear glass pedestal, and with no apparent attachments. Psycho was a magician who could guess a word chosen by a spectator, guess the correct answer to a sum, indicate the value of a chosen card, or play a game of whist with three spectators. No authentic explanation has ever been given, though ingenious ideas have been offered. He is now to be seen in the London Museum.

psychokinesis. Also PK (abbreviation) or telekinesis. Supposed influence exerted on the movement of an object without its being physically touched. Of dubious authenticity, but frequently simulated by conjurers with good effect. *ESP*.

pull. *Gimmick* enabling articles varying in size from a billiard ball to a folded bird-cage to be swiftly dragged out of sight under the performer's clothes. One type consists of a length of elastic attached at one end to the back of the performer's belt or braces, coming down his sleeve and ending in a pear- or ball-shaped container or a nylon loop; *illustration 122*. Another form of pull has one end of a cord attached to (say) his left wrist or elbow, whence it goes across his back and down the other sleeve, where it ends in some kind of fastener to be attached to the object; *illustration 17*. If both arms are thrown outwards simultaneously the pull will instantly draw the object up the right sleeve. *Bird-cage, Vanishing*. See Hay, *AMATEUR MAGICIAN'S HANDBOOK*, pp.247–9; Hugard, *MODERN MAGIC MANUAL*, p.189.

122. Pull attached to elastic. End marked A is attached to belt.

Q

quick-change magic. Change of costume and appearance (sometimes sex) carried out in a few seconds. An effective one is the change of a man in overcoat and evening suit to a lady in full evening dress. Shirt, collar, etc., are attached to the overcoat, and by removing this the man removes at the same time all the rest of his upper clothing. Under it he is wearing lady's evening dress, and the fall of the (weighted) skirt automatically hides his trousers. A lady's wig completes the change. Carried out behind a screen or within a cabinet it can be presented as a *transformation* illusion. Some performers have specialized in the art. *Lafayette* used to appear as an artist, a Chinese magician, and a military bandsman, with almost instantaneous changes. One of the most famous quick-change artists was Charles Aldrich, an American who appeared at the first Royal Command performance (London, 1912).

quickness. The popular belief that in magic 'the quickness of the hand deceives the eye' is a fallacy. Lightning speed is rarely a main factor in magical deception, which depends far more on *misdirection*.

R

rabbit. The production of a rabbit from a top hat is sometimes used to symbolize magic, although it is not an old trick, a good one, or one frequently performed. (The *Cups and Balls* or *Linking Rings* would be a better symbol.) The rabbit is usually bundled into a bag and hidden behind a chair or inside a jacket, waiting to be *loaded*. Symbolic pictures usually show the rabbit being lifted from the hat by the ears, which should never be done. The animal should be held at the back of the neck and supported underneath. If a rabbit is produced in a faked *production box* it should have plenty of space and air while lying concealed in the hidden compartment. A rabbit should not be presented to a child at the end of a trick. The owning of pets is a responsibility to be entered into only after careful consideration. *Run, Rabbit, Run*.

Ramsay, John (1877–1962). Scottish amateur magician generally regarded as one of the greatest close-up sleight-of-hand performers, with a considerable influence on this branch of magic. See Andrew Galloway, THE RAMSAY LEGEND (1969, 1975); THE RAMSAY CLASSICS (1978).

Randi, James (James Randall Zwinge). Canadian escapologist who began his magical career as assistant to a travelling magician, joined a circus, and then decided to specialize in *mentalism*, calling himself 'The Great Randall Telepath'. Changing his name to 'The Amazing Randi', he went to the U.S.A., where he followed to some extent in the footsteps of *Houdini*, both as an escaper and as a debunker of phoney psychics. His exposures of *Geller* have become notable.

Rapping Hand, The. Wax hand which, after being examined, is placed preferably on a sheet of glass. Thus isolated it can tap out the answers to spectators' questions, rapping once for 'No' and twice or thrice for 'Yes'; *illustration 123*. It is usually actuated by the tightening of a thread stretched across the cuff. A talking skull, which 'speaks' by rocking noisily backwards and forwards, is also often actuated by a thread, though sometimes by magnetism.

rattle bars. Three little wooden or metal bars used for a form of *three-card trick*. One is hollow and rattles when shaken. The victim is invited to guess which it is and is shown to be wrong when the performer picks up one of the others and apparently rattles it. The secret is a palmed duplicate rattling bar. Other articles (e.g. small bells) are sometimes used. There is also a similar trick with matchboxes, the secret box being hidden (though often somewhat muffled) in the performer's sleeve.

Razor-blade Trick. *Needle Trick*.

readers. *marked cards*.

reel. Small *gimmick* for automatically winding a thread on to a drum, and used for the mysterious tying and untying of *silks*, or for *Rising* cards, etc. It may be held in the fingers or

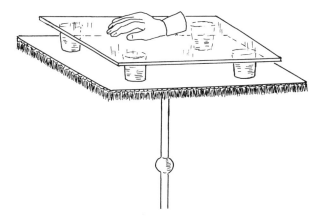

123. Rapping hand isolated on glass.

attached to the arm or clothing. See Robinson, *MAGIC AS A PASTIME*, p.54.

rehearsal. *practice.*

repeat. *Six Card Repeat.*

reversed card. (1) Card that is back to front in the pack (e.g. face up while the rest are face down), or (2) card turned upside down in a *one-way pack.* This double meaning of 'reversed' can sometimes cause confusion. It would be better in the second instance to use the term 'upside-down card'.

reversed fan. *Fan* of cards made anti-clockwise, so that the indexes are hidden and the cards (especially A, 2, 3) appear blank. A nudist or reversed card should cover the printing on the front card.

ribbon fountain. From a round tin or vase a long broad ribbon comes streaming like a fountain of water. Many laymen imagine that the effect is mechanical, with a clockwork mechanism unwinding the ribbon. It is, however, produced by careful preliminary pleating of the ribbon, which may be anything up to a couple of hundred yards long. The display is attractive and colourful rather than mysterious. First shown in Britain by *Kovari.*

ribbon spread. Line of cards after *spreading.*

Rice Bowls. Classic trick often known as Chinese, though it is probably Indian in origin. Two bowls are exhibited. One is then filled with rice; the bowls are placed mouth to mouth, and after they have been secretly inverted the rice is found to have doubled in quantity. The surplus rice is scooped off, the bowls are put together again, and this time the rice is found to have changed to water. One bowl is in fact already filled with water, prevented from escaping by a rice-covered metal plate or a plastic disc. The disc is secretly removed when the excess rice is scooped off with a napkin. Another version has Indian bowls made of spun brass, one of them shallow, with a (punctured) false bottom and with water in the lower part; *illustration 124.* A modern version uses glass or plastic tumblers in

121

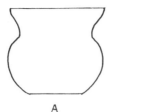
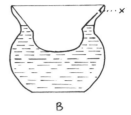

124. Indian Rice Bowls. When B is inverted, water trickles through at X into A, the rice sinking to the bottom.

125. A modern version of the Rice Bowls with tumblers.

place of bowls; *illustration 125*. See Elliott, *CLASSIC SECRETS OF MAGIC*, pp.133–9; Gibson, *HOUDINI'S MAGIC*, pp.102–4.

riffle. Action with playing-cards (sometimes also known as ruffle) employed to mislead spectators. The fingers are drawn sharply upward against one end of the pack (which is held in the other hand or pressed against the table), allowing the cards to spring back with a crisp flicking noise; *illustration 126*. The action suggests some magical move, but in fact it has no effect at all and requires no skill, though spectators may be induced to believe that it is the cause of (say) a card's mysteri-

126. The riffle.

ous disappearance.

rigged. *faked.*

Ring on Wand. A borrowed ring is apparently wrapped in a handkerchief but really *switched* for one that is lightly sewn to the handkerchief. A spectator holds this, while the performer, secretly sliding the borrowed ring on to a thin wand or stick, has the two ends held by another spectator. Taking the handkerchief and draping it over the wand, he gives it a sudden pull, revealing that the ring is now spinning on the wand. There are various other ways of performing the trick, which is probably Indian in origin. See Warlock, *COMPLETE BOOK OF MAGIC*, pp.19–21.

Rising Cards. Very popular trick, dating from the eighteenth century and performed in literally dozens of different ways. Three or four spectators each select a card; these are replaced in the pack and then asked or commanded to rise out of it, which they do in turn. The simplicity and straightforwardness of the routine is one reason for its success. The standard method is for a thread to run under each chosen card and over the cards immediately before and behind it; *illustrations 127, 127a.* Thus a steady pull on the thread (by a hidden assistant) lifts each card. Alternatively the end of the thread may be fastened to the table, the cards rising when the per-

127. The Rising Cards: thread method.

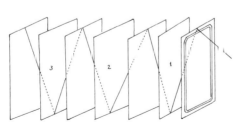

127a. The Rising Cards: arrangement of the thread, with rear of pack on right.

Robert-Houdin, Jean

former tightens the thread by moving slightly forward. Other methods involve human hairs, elastic bands, sleight-of-hand, clockwork, pulley wheels, and other mechanical devices. The cards are variously placed in special holders (*houlettes*), glass tumblers, goblets, card cases, or simply held in the hand. Sleight-of-hand methods depend primarily on bringing the cards to the top of the pack and making them rise by finger action. One of the best mechanical packs is the Devano, which consists mainly of ordinary cards. *GREATER MAGIC* devotes nearly 50 pages to the trick, the *TARBELL COURSE* nearly 40. Less exhaustive treatment is in Gibson, *WHAT'S NEW IN MAGIC*, pp.216–18; Robinson, *MAGIC AS A PASTIME*, pp.37–8.

Robert-Houdin, Jean (1805–71). French magician generally regarded as the Father of Modern Magic. The son of a watchmaker, he followed the same trade, though his father wanted him to be a lawyer. Later he married the daughter of a celebrated watchmaker named Houdin and legally added the name to his own. Much of his time was devoted to making and repairing automata. In 1845 he opened his own Theatre of Magic in Paris. Three years later he toured England successfully; *illustration 128*. After only a short professional career he retired, but in 1856 he accepted a government invitation to visit French Algeria to counter the influence of rebellious native sorcerers. His *MEMOIRS* (1859), basically true, are a little romanticized but offer delightful reading, and his conjuring textbooks, *SECRETS OF CONJURING AND MAGIC* (1868) and *SECRETS OF STAGE CONJURING* (1877), trans-

lated by *Hoffmann*, are (especially the former) among the great magical classics. Among his most impressive feats was the *Second Sight* act that he developed with his eldest son, Emile. His influence in fostering the artistic presentation of magic cannot seriously be questioned. The attack on his reputation by *Houdini* boomeranged on its author. *Sharpe, S. H.*

Robin, Henri (Henri-Joseph Dunkell, (c.1805–75). Dutch-born conjurer who called himself 'The French Wizard' and based his magical career in France. A performer of some distinction, he entertained royalty and public in several European countries; in England he appeared for a while at the *Egyptian Hall*. Like *Robert-Houdin*, with whom there was a certain rivalry, he was also interested in electricity and optics. He claimed to have invented the *Ghost Trick* principle before Dircks and *Pepper*, but he failed to exploit its potentiality to the full. One of his notable tricks was The Medium of Inkerman, a ghostly invisible drummer who tapped answers to spectators' questions; *illustration 94*.

Robinson, William Ellsworth. *Chung Ling Soo.*

Rooklyn, Maurice. Experienced Australian magician who toured Britain before the last war with a skilful manipulative act. He presented a big magic show in Australia, and a sensational *Bullet Catch* routine. He is a specialist in billiard-ball sleight-of-hand, and author (with *Ganson*) of *SPHERICAL SORCERY* (1973), partly autobiographical.

rope cement. Substance for joining together two ends of rope. Applied to an obliquely cut rope and allowed

ROBERT-HOUDIN,

ST. JAMES'S THEATRE.

The celebrated M. ROBERT-HOUDIN will continue his Incredible
Delusions and Extraordinary

FANTASTIQUES

AT THE ABOVE THEATRE,

EVERY

TUESDAY,

THURSDAY,

AND

SATURDAY

EVENINGS,

Doors open at Eight o'clock.

LE FAVORI DES DAMES

A GRAND

DAY

PERFORMANCE

EVERY

WEDNESDAY

MORNING,

Commencing at Half-past Two o'clock.

Houdin's Original Delusions.

The Programme will comprise a Selection from Robert-Houdin's Original Experiments and
Extraordinary Wonders, in addition to several New and Startling Novelties, including

THE MIRACULOUS BALANCE,

THE INEXHAUSTIBLE BOTTLE,

SECOND SIGHT,   INVISIBILÉTÉ,

AND

SUSPENSION ÉTHÉRÉENNE.

BOXES, 4s.   PIT, 2s.   AMPHITHEATRE, 1s. 6d.

PRIVATE BOXES, ORCHESTRA STALLS, AND TICKETS, MAY BE SECURED AT
MR. MITCHELL'S ROYAL LIBRARY, 33, OLD BOND STREET,
Mr. Sams' Royal Library, St. James's Street; Messrs. Ebers', Hookham's, Allcroft's, Andrews', Leader and Cock's, Chappell's, and Ollivier's Libraries, Bond street;
Cramer's, and the Carlton Library, 12, Regent Street;
And at the BOX OFFICE of the Theatre, which is open Daily, from Eleven till Five o'clock.

PRINTED BY W. J. GOLBOURN, 6 PRINCES STREET, LEICESTER SQUARE.

128. Robert-Houdin: poster for a
London performance. ('Victorian
Magic', No. 12.)

to dry, it will fix the two ends almost invisibly when they are pressed together, usually in a cut and restored rope effect. Obtainable from magic dealers.

Rope, Cut and Restored. Very popular trick with many magicians, based on the *Cut and Restored String*. There are broadly three possible methods: (1) an end instead of the middle is cut, as in the C. and R. String; (2) an extra piece of rope is secretly introduced, and is cut instead of the real length of rope; (3) rope cement or patent fasteners are used to join the severed ends in secret. The *TARBELL COURSE*, Vol. 2 deals extensively with rope tricks, including c. and r. methods. For simpler treatment see Reed, *MAGICAL MIRACLES YOU CAN DO*, pp.56–7; Baron, *MAGIC SIMPLIFIED*, p.74, *CLOSE-UP MAGIC FOR BEGINNERS*, pp.42–8; Scarne, *SCARNE'S MAGIC TRICKS*, pp.66–7.

rope stretching. The magician shows a piece of rope two or three feet long. It appears ordinary, but suddenly it begins to grow longer and longer until it is three or four times its original length. The secret is an extra piece of rope concealed within the performer's clothes and running down his sleeve; it is pulled out as though part of the piece first shown. See *GREATER MAGIC*, pp.794–7, which also describes a method using a single piece of rope.

Rope Trick, Indian. *Indian Rope Trick.*

Ropes and Rings. Really the *Grandmother's Necklace* trick on a larger scale. Ropes are substituted for string and curtain rings for beads. The join is usually hidden by passing the ropes through the sleeves of a borrowed jacket. A single knot is then tied with the double ropes, and the ends are held by two spectators. Two or more rings are now put on the ropes and pushed down to the knot, after which a single knot is tied, taking *one end* of rope from each spectator. Jacket and rings can now be freed if the performer breaks the join and gets the spectators holding the ends to pull. See Devant, *LESSONS IN CONJURING*, pp.109–21.

Rosini, Carl (John Rosen, *b* 1882). As a youth he came to England from Poland in order to learn magic. Both here and in Germany he developed into a fine performer, but he finally settled in the U.S.A. He originated a good many tricks of his own, but his outstanding feat was the *Thumb Tie*, taught him by Ten Ichi, the Japanese magician. His life story was written by Robert Olson (1966).

rough-and-smooth principle. Important development in card conjuring technique introduced by Ralph W. Hull before the last war, though *Hoffmann* had touched on the basic idea 20 years earlier. It involves 'roughing' one side of a playing-card by the application of some adhesive (*roughing fluid*) and 'smoothing' the other side by polishing (*slick card*). Some remarkable tricks can be performed with cards thus treated (e.g. *Brainwave pack*). The technique is fully dealt with in *Hall's NOTHING IS IMPOSSIBLE*, but it is an artifice for the expert rather than the neophyte.

roughing fluid. Chemical substance which causes playing-cards to adhere to each other temporarily, so that two cards can easily be shown as one, though they may be separated by pressure. Available from magic dealers. *rough-and-smooth principle.*

routine. Either (1) the sequence of moves or actions performed during a single trick (e.g. *Linking Rings*) or

(2) a coherent arrangement of tricks, each one leading naturally to the next.

running gag. Trick that is repeated again and again at intervals during a performer's act, the repetition often turning an otherwise serious trick into a comedy item. *Kalanag* would from time to time empty a large *Lota vase* into a bucket, gravely explaining 'Water from India' each time. Larry Parker, a clever English comedy conjurer, uses a brandy flask in a somewhat similar way.

Run, Rabbit, Run. Classic children's *sucker* trick on the lines of the *sliding die box*, and roughly the same size. Two doors are separated by a wall. A cut-out rabbit keeps moving from door to door 'unnoticed' by the performer, while children shout the information with ear-splitting excitement; *illustration 129*.

ruse. Deceptive *move*, usually achieved by *misdirection*.

Russian Roulette. Type of *Gun Trick*, featured by *Fogel*. Five air-guns in a rack hold bullets, but a sixth is empty. Five spectators choose a gun and shoot, their bullets shattering five plates. The sixth shoots at the performer, and his gun (all being well) turns out to be the empty one. But the trick has its dangers. Fogel has been injured once or twice, and in 1974 a South African was shot in the stomach and seriously wounded. In the same year an American magician was killed during a rehearsal. *Bullet Catch*.

129. Run, Rabbit, Run.

S

sack escapes. Popular form of escape trick, either in conjunction with a *box trick* or as a separate item. There are various methods, one of the most ingenious being to leave a gap in the hem containing the long cord with which the mouth of the sack is fastened. As soon as the performer is enclosed in the sack (which can be previously examined) he pulls down a foot or two of cord; *illustration 130*. When a spectator has tied the mouth of the sack and sealed the knot, under an assistant's

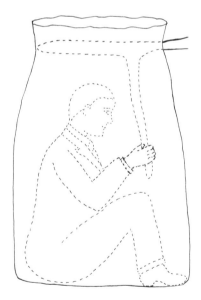

130. Sack escape: cord pulled down from inside.

directions, a screen is placed in front. The performer now releases the loop he has pulled down, and this provides an opening wide enough for him to get through. The loose cord is knotted and tucked into the hem, leaving the spectator's sealed knot untouched. There are various other methods. See Adair, *CONJURING AS A CRAFT*, pp.129–33; Devant, *TRICKS FOR EVERYONE*, pp.111–13.

St George's Hall. London theatre devoted solely to magic, 1905–33. When his lease of the *Egyptian Hall* was expiring, *J. N. Maskelyne* bought St George's Hall in Langham Place, almost rebuilt it, and opened it as his new Home of Mystery on 2 January, 1905, with a magic play, *THE COMING RACE*. This was not a success, but with a more traditional magic programme St George's Hall remained England's Home of Mystery for nearly 30 years. In 1933 it was sold to the BBC and ceased to be the home of magic, to the regret of all magic devotees.

S.A.M. *Society of American Magicians*.

sand frame. Apparatus for revealing a card that has previously been vanished. The glass of a small picture frame is double. When the frame is placed one way up a thin layer of sand comes between the two sheets of glass and gives the impression that the frame is empty. Turned the other way up under cover of a handkerchief, the frame allows the sand to trickle out of sight, leaving a duplicate of the vanished card revealed. *card frame*.

Sand Trick. *Coloured Sands*.

Sawing a Woman in Half. The most popular illusion of modern times, originated by *Selbit* in 1921. In his earliest version the victim was completely enclosed in a coffin-like box which was cut in half with a big saw;

illustration 131. The idea was taken up in America by *Goldin*, who devised a different method. Since then a great many performers have cut their victims in half in various ways. One innovation has been the introduction of a buzz saw which appears to cut through the victim without even the protection of a box. Dramatic impact is stressed by

131. The original Sawing a Woman in Half, performed by Selbit.

some performers. Goldin had an ambulance in the street and a nurse and stretcher in the theatre lobby. Richiardi, a Peruvian performer, spatters blood all over the place and invites dozens of spectators to view the apparent disembowelment – realism which is not everyone's form of entertainment. Other performers relieve the tension by introducing comedy. There are many methods of performing the trick, one of the original devices being to allow the victim's middle to sink through a trap in the box and table. Sometimes two girls are used. See Gibson, SECRETS OF THE GREAT MAGICIANS, pp.112–14; PROFESSIONAL MAGIC FOR AMATEURS, pp.183–7.

'The Scarab'. Magical playlet first produced by *Maskelyne and Devant* in 1910 at *St George's Hall*. A magic charm in the form of a scarab (sacred beetle) brings to life the mummy of an ancient Egyptian king, with various mystical results, including strange appearances and disappearances from boxes and cabinets. It was revived more than once with great success.

Scarne, John (Orlando Scarnecchia). American sleight-of-hand conjurer, generally regarded as the leading authority on gambling methods. An expert conjurer in many fields, notably dice, cards, and figures, and a forthright debunker of credulous beliefs and fraudulent claims in *ESP*, hypnotism, etc. SCARNE ON DICE (1945) and SCARNE ON CARDS (1956) are definitive works, and his conjuring books, SCARNE ON CARD TRICKS (1950) and SCARNE'S MAGIC TRICKS (1951) are full of material suitable for beginners.

Scot, Reginald (1538–99). Author of THE DISCOVERIE OF WITCHCRAFT.

Seabrooke, Terry. Experienced and amusing professional conjurer who draws his humour from situation rather than gags and jokes. He gives his own individual and comic version of standard tricks such as the *Chinese Sticks* and *Sawing a Woman in Half.*

second deal. Card sleight in which the performer deals the second card from the top instead of the top card. *false deal.*

second sight. Ancient belief, in Scottish and other Celtic folklore, that things distant in place or time can be seen as if they were present. Dr Johnson made investigations while in the Scottish Highlands, without coming to any definite conclusion. Conjurers have used the term to cover the kind of thought-reading in which the performer apparently transmits mental impressions of an object, word, number, etc., to his assistant or *medium*. *Robert-Houdin* was probably the first conjurer to make a great feature of this, though his claim to have invented it is a little exaggerated. *Pinetti.*

secret. The means, unknown to the audience, by which a trick is performed. *exposure.*

secretly. (1) Without being observed by the audience. (2) Without the performer being able to see (as applied to a spectator writing a word or looking at a card).

Selbit, P. T. (Percy Tibbles, 1879–1938). Magical inventor, performer, and journalist with probably the most fertile magical mind of his period. Dozens of his illusions were performed, by himself and by innumerable copyists. Many of his ingenious inventions involved the apparent maltreatment of young lady assistants, who were stretched, crushed, and (in the most famous of all his tricks) almost visibly sawn in half; *illustration 131*. As well as performing under his usual pseudonym he sometimes appeared as Joad Heteb, an Egyptian 'Wizard of the Sphinx'. When *The Wizard* was started in 1905 (*magazines*) Selbit was its editor; he was also a columnist for *THE SHOWMAN*. His books (e.g. *THE MAGICIAN'S HANDBOOK*, 1901) are not without interest but they tend to be scrappy.

selected card. Card chosen by a spectator in the course of a trick.

self-working trick. One that needs no digital skill. But no trick, however easy to perform, is really self-working, for the essential thing is the performer's ability to present it in such a way that it both mystifies and entertains.

servante. Hidden shelf or receptacle (especially popular with Victorian magicians) for *ditching* or *stealing* articles. Many are made of strong net; some have a small shelf which can be raised or lowered. Servantes are usually hidden behind a cloth-covered table or a suitable chair: if this is open at the back, then a scarf

132. Servante for switching a pack of cards, fixed to the back of a chair.

or newspaper is firmly pinned to hide the gap. A servante to change a pack of cards has a clip to hold the new pack and a net to receive the old one; *illustration 132*.

set-up. *Prearrangement* of a pack of cards.

Sharpe, S. H. Writer on magical theory (e.g. *NEO-MAGIC*, 1932, 1946) and history. His most important work is *SALUTATIONS TO ROBERT-HOUDIN*, a detailed historical survey serialized in *THE LINKING RING*, 1967–74.

Shaxon, Alan. Clever magical entertainer, formerly in banking. Becoming a professional magician many years ago, he now presents a slick act for cabaret or private concerts, often assisted by his wife, Anne. His methods and ideas are clearly revealed in *MY KIND OF MAGIC* (1970) and *PRACTICAL SORCERY* (1977).

shadowgraphy. The art of making shadows for amusement, primarily with the hands, though sometimes accessories are added.

shell. Hollow covering or half-covering which fits closely over an article such as a ball, coin, or die, and exactly resembles it in appearance. Thus one ball or coin can be made to change suddenly into two by deftly sliding the solid one from behind the shell. Conversely, a solid one slipped into a shell will appear to have vanished. *ball box*; *billiard balls*.

shift. Term sometimes used by American magicians for the *pass with cards*.

Shimada, Haruo. Leading Japanese magician from Tokyo, whose club and stage acts with his Australian wife, Deanna, have been greatly admired in many countries, especially the U.S.A. In the theatre he fea-

131

tures the production of innumerable brightly coloured umbrellas, completely filling the whole stage with them.

short card. Card a fraction shorter than the rest of the pack, thus easily found by touch and useful as a *locator card*.

showmanship. Whole books have been written on magical showmanship. Briefly it is the art of making a favourable impression on the audience and of giving such significance to each trick that the spectators never lose interest. Among the many factors involved are the performer's voice and personality, his rapport with the audience, his choice and combination of tricks, and his ability to give an individual touch to the whole routine. These things are partly inherent but can partly be acquired. Among the books dealing with the subject are: Fitzkee, *SHOWMANSHIP FOR MAGICIANS* (1943); Edward Maurice, *SHOWMANSHIP AND PRESENTATION* (1968); Masoni, *SHOWMANSHIP OUT OF THE HAT* (1970); Henning Nelms, *MAGIC AND SHOWMANSHIP* (1969), perhaps the best book of its kind, with very precise examples and detail.

shuffle. Act of mixing up cards. *false s.; Faro s.; Hindu s.; overhand s.; riffle s.; dovetail s.*

Si Stebbins (Will H. Coffrin). American originator of a well-known card *set-up*. What is generally known as the Si Stebbins system has the cards arranged in numerical order, each one three away from its neighbours, and with the suits rotating C, H, S, D. For example: 3C, 6H, 9S, QD, 2C, 5H, 8S, JD, etc. In fact, however, Stebbins himself did not use this arrangement but had his cards *four* numbers apart: e.g. 3S, 7C, JH,

2D, 6S, 10C, AH, etc., with a different rotation of suits.

side steal. Advanced sleight whereby a card in the middle of the pack is marked by a *break* and then pushed sideways into the palm of the hand covering the pack. See Gibson, *COMPLETE ILLUSTRATED BOOK OF CARD MAGIC*, pp.174–5.

signal. Method by which a performer communicates with his partner or *medium* in a mind-reading act. *code*.

sightless vision. The ability to see despite having the eyes completely covered. *blindfold*.

silent act. Performance given without *patter*, often to music, sometimes presented in oriental costume. Though it may be humorous or semi-humorous, as in *Cardini*'s act, it more often attempts to be mysterious, and may involve showy, colourful productions of silks, flags, bouquets, etc. *Manipulations* are often performed without patter. A shy, soft-voiced beginner may find a silent act helpful, but *misdirection* is much harder to achieve without speech.

silks. Conjurer's term for handkerchiefs, as those used for *productions*, etc., are made of thin silk, which compresses into a very small space. Silks for production should not be too skimpy, however, or they will look ridiculous from a distance. Spectators naturally know silks as handkerchiefs or scarves, and these terms should be used when addressing an audience. See Hugard, *MODERN MAGIC MANUAL*, pp 177–210.

'Sim Sala Bim'. Title of *Dante*'s magic show, later adopted by *Kalanag*. *magic words*.

simulation. Imitation of an action that is supposed to be taking place. It must be convincingly done. For instance, when an apple or ball is supposed to be held in a hand which is really empty, the closed fist must not be too firmly clenched. It should copy exactly the shape of the hand when a ball is really held. *misdirection.*

Six-Card Repeat. Six cards are counted by the performer. Three of them are tossed aside, yet there are still six remaining. The same process is repeated several times, and each time there appear to be just six cards. The secret lies in *false counting.* There are usually 16 to 18 cards altogether, but with the *fifth* card (each time) the remaining cards are pushed off and counted as a single card. Barefaced though this seems, the trick is a very effective one when well presented. Special cards can be obtained from some dealers to simplify the working. See Gibson, *COMPLETE ILLUSTRATED BOOK OF CARD MAGIC*, pp.205–9; Clive, *CARD TRICKS WITHOUT SKILL*, pp.127–8.

skill. Normally used by conjurers with reference to the ability to carry out *manipulations* with small articles smoothly and dexterously. But the term also applies to the effective use of *misdirection. sleight-of-hand.*

Skull, Talking. *Rapping Hand.*

slate. Still used by many conjurers, especially in *mentalism*, though condemned by others as being an old-fashioned article no longer in everyday use. Lay audiences, however, rarely appear to look on the slate as out-of-date, perhaps because it is so obviously useful. A word clearly written in chalk on a slate can be seen at the back of a large hall. A slate offers a firm writing surface; moreover, words and figures can easily be erased when necessary. Slate tricks are often based on spirit medium practices and consist in having a word, message, or number mysteriously written on a slate surface previously shown blank. The secret is usually a *slate-flap*, or a *switch of slates*, or the use of a *nail-writer*. Chemical methods are also occasionally employed. Conjurers' slates are normally made of board, bakelite, or some such substance. Miniature pocket-slates are used in some tricks. See Elliott, *MAGIC AS A HOBBY*, pp.199–219; Warlock, *THE BEST TRICKS WITH SLATES* (1942).

slate-flap. Sheet of black cardboard, etc., closely resembling the surface of a *slate*, and fitting exactly into the frame. If the flap is placed over a word or message written on one side of a slate, the latter appears free from writing. With the flap secretly released (e.g. inside a paper bag), the writing is revealed. Slates are often used in pairs, with the flap passing from one slate to the other and thus revealing the writing; *illustration 133.*

133. Slates and slate-flap.

sleeving. Some expert conjurers have begun to revive the old-fashioned use of the sleeve for vanishing small articles. The article should be allowed to slide easily into the sleeve of a slightly raised arm while seemingly held in the other hand. The move should be used sparingly.

sleight. Dexterous action with any small article, either for utility (e.g. *pass*) or as a *flourish*.

sleight-of-hand. Skill in using the hands (mainly for purposes of deception) in entertainment or gambling, normally with cards, coins, balls, cigarettes, thimbles, and similar small objects. *manipulation; quickness; pass; palm; false count, deal, shuffle; flourish*.

'Sleight of Hand'. Classic conjuring book (1877) which together with *MODERN MAGIC* had a great influence in developing interest in conjuring and skill in performance. The author, Edwin T. Sachs, a London sporting journalist, laid less stress on apparatus than *Hoffmann* had done and more stress on skill and *misdirection*. A fifth edition was published in 1953.

slick card. One with a polished surface, enabling the pack to be easily cut at this card. Car polish can be used for the purpose.

sliding die box. *die box, sliding*.

slip. Simple *sleight* useful as a *force*. *Knife force*.

Slydini, Tony (Quintino Marucci). Italian magician resident in America since early youth. Inspired by his father, an amateur magician, he started conjuring early in life, at one time performing as 'Tony Foolem', later adopting his present pseudonym. His great reputation as a master of sleight-of-hand and misdirection in close-up magic is largely based on his performances in private engagements and on his skill as a teacher of magic.

societies, magical. The oldest magical society in Britain is the British Magical Society, Birmingham (March 1905). The *Magic Circle*, London,

followed a few months later (July 1905). Within the next few years other societies appeared in various parts of the country. They included the Northern Magical Society, Liverpool (1908); the Order of the Magi, Manchester (1909); the Associated Wizards of the South, Southampton (1911); the Mahatma Circle of Magicians, Liverpool (1914); the North Western Society of Magicians (1915); the Leeds Magical Society (1919); the Sheffield Circle of Magicians (1920); the Scottish Conjurers' Association (1924); the Leicester Magic Circle (1924). A great many others have sprung up within the last 50 years, and now there are nearly 100 in the U.K. Reports of some of their meetings are recorded in *ABRACADABRA* from time to time. Anyone seriously interested in conjuring should consider joining a convenient society, where his interest in the art of magic will be encouraged and fostered by fellow-conjurers and by the talks and demonstrations which most societies include in their programme. A local paper or library would probably indicate the nearest magical society. Failing this, the editor of *ABRACADABRA* would no doubt offer advice, given a stamped addressed envelope. *I.B.M.; British Ring; Society of American Magicians*. See Vintus, *MAGICIANS OF THE WORLD* (1978).

Society of American Magicians. Probably the oldest magical society extant, founded in May 1902, three years before the two earliest surviving British societies. It had its origin in a meeting of a handful of magicians in a New York magic store. Within six months there were nearly 100 members. Now there are several thousand members, with the Parent Assembly in New York and branches in over 60 cities. Its motto is 'Magic, Unity, Might', and its monthly journal is entitled *M.U.M.*

Sorcar, P. C. (1913–71). Famous and much publicized Indian magician, who presented in the main a Western-type show with some Indian colouring. If not 'The World's Greatest Magician', as he styled himself, he developed into a fine performer with an impressive full evening show which he took all over the world. In England in 1956 his buzz-saw 'severing' of a girl assistant created a sensation on TV when the trick was faded out through lack of time before the girl had been restored. Sorcar died from a heart attack in Japan at the age of 57; his body received an impressive funeral in India. His second son, Sorcar Junior, took over the magic show and presents an equally impressive and colourful evening's entertainment. *SORCAR ON MAGIC* (1960), published in Calcutta, is a finely produced book.

Speller. Short for Spelling Trick, in which the identity of a chosen card is spelt by dealing a card for each letter of the name. The chosen card itself is turned up either as the last card of the spelling or as the following card. Variations include spelling the spectator's (or someone else's) name. The *Spelling Bee* is another form of Speller. See Hugard, *ENCYCLOPEDIA OF CARD TRICKS*, pp.45–73; Gibson, *PROFESSIONAL MAGIC FOR AMATEURS*, pp.41–5; Anderson, *MAGICAL DIGEST*, pp.60–2. Clive, *Card Tricks Without Skill*, p.185.

Spelling Bee. In this card trick all the values are spelt in turn, from a-c-e to q-u-e-e-n, a card being slipped from top to bottom of a 13-card packet at each letter. As each value is spelt, the next card is placed on the table and proves to be a card of the value just spelt. The packet of 13 cards gradually diminishes in size until only the king is left. The cards should be arranged in order: 3, 8, 7, A, Q, 6, 4, 2, J, K, 10, 9, 5. The trick is then *self-working*. See Lamb, *YOUR BOOK OF CARD TRICKS*, pp.28–9; Scarne, *SCARNE ON CARD TRICKS*, pp.118–19.

Sphinx, The. Stage illusion first produced in 1865 at the *Egyptian Hall* by Colonel *Stodare*. On a small table he placed a square box which he said contained the head of an old Egyptian magician. The Sphinx-like head was obviously alive, and answered questions freely. Yet no body was visible. The trick was an optical illusion based on the *mirror principle*; the body of a man beneath the table was hidden by two mirrors. When the (bottomless) box was placed on the table he pushed up his head through a trap.

'Sphinx, The'. Famous American magical magazine founded in March 1902 as 'An Independent Magazine for Magicians'. The *S.A.M.* used its columns for many years for reports, etc. Its first editor was outspoken Dr A. M. Wilson; its last *John Mulholland*. It ceased publication in 1953.

spider. Apparatus for simplifying the *back-palming* of a coin, though it has never been widely used. A swivelling coin has two small clips which are held by the first and fourth fingers, enabling the coin to be back-palmed without danger of its falling; *illustration 134*. Spiders for other articles also have been devised; *illustration 135*.

sponge balls. Balls made from sponge rubber, natural sponge, or nylon

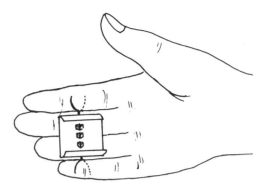

134. Coin spider.

135. Spider for back-palming small articles.

foam, hence very compressible and often used in close-up magic. They can be bought from dealers or cut to shape from a bath sponge. Sizes vary, but about two inches (5 cm) in diameter is common. Sponge ball routines include the usual vanishes and reappearances, but the special feature of sponge is that a spectator can hold two balls in his clenched fist under the belief that there is only one (or three believed to be two). Thus a ball can be vanished and made to pass mysteriously into his closed hand. Many variations are possible. Sponges may also be used for a *Cups and Balls* routine. For sponge routines see Hugard, *MODERN MAGIC MANUAL*, pp.138–45; Page, *BIG BOOK OF MAGIC*, pp.115–24; Reed, *MAGICAL MIRACLES YOU CAN DO*, pp.39–41.

spreading the cards. Spreading a pack of cards along the table so that they lie in a long line (straight or curved) with a small portion of each card showing. Generally used as a *flourish*, which is completed by turning the end card over and thus reversing the whole line. A more advanced flourish is to spread them along the inside of one arm, from elbow to fingers. See Baron, *CARD TRICKS FOR BEGINNERS*, pp.51–2; Hugard, *MODERN MAGIC MANUAL*, pp. 351–2.

spring flowers. Artificial flowers which can be compressed into a very small space but which open up through a spring action when produced from a box, hat, or cone. Invented by *De Kolta*.

springing the cards. Card flourish. The performer holds the cards in the right hand, pressing with the thumb at the bottom, first and second fingers at the top, with the pack bulging towards the palm. If the cards are released evenly, one at a time, they should spring to the other hand. A good deal of practice is necessary.

square the cards. Tidy the edges of a pack of cards.

Square Circle Box. Production box consisting of a decorated cylindrical tube inside a square box with an open-work front. The tube and box in turn are shown unmistakably empty and replaced. *Silks*, sweets, or other articles, according to the size of the box, can now be immediately produced from the apparently empty tube. The secret is an inner tube, painted black to match the inside of the box and thus invisible through the open-work when the brightly decorated outer tube is raised to be shown empty.

square, magic. *magic square.*

Squaring the Circle. A circle of metal changes suddenly to a square. Obviously mechanical and thus surprising rather than mysterious.

Squircle. A circle is cut in a sheet of newspaper, but when the paper is opened the circle has become a square.

stacked pack. *prearranged pack.*

Stanley, Harry. Experienced professional conjurer and dealer, who retired in 1970. His Unique Magic Studio in London's West End was for many years a leading magic store. Publisher of *THE GEN* magazine and of many important magical books.

Stanyon, Ellis (1871–1951). For many years a prominent London (Hampstead) magical dealer, teacher, and writer; founder of the first British magical journal, *MAGIC* (1900); *illustration 94*. Although he seems to have made little mark as a performer, he was a prolific and versatile writer on magic. His score of booklets known as *SERIALS* (1899–1911) gave instruction on every branch of magical entertainment. A comprehensive 'Dictionary of Magical Effects' was serialized in *MAGIC* from 1911 onwards, and every issue also included a detailed 'Original Lesson in Magic'. He compiled, with help, a bibliography of conjuring, incomplete but a valuable pioneer work, and was the author of *CONJURING FOR AMATEURS* (1897) and *CONJURING*

WITH CARDS (1898).

steal. To secure an article secretly, without the audience knowing.

Stickland, William. Secretary of the *British Ring* of the I.B.M. and the driving force behind it for over 40 years; an estate agent in private life. The first Englishman to be appointed International President of the I.B.M. (1971). Awarded the M.B.E. in 1978 for services to magic.

Stillwell ball. Hollow ball with a hole in one side, used for vanishing or producing handkerchiefs. The ball is kept out of sight by sleight-of-hand. Its innovator was George Stillwell, an American specialist in handkerchief magic at the turn of the century. *handkerchief ball.* See Hugard, *MODERN MAGIC MANUAL*, pp.201–4.

stock. Batch of cards kept together for some purpose, especially during shuffling.

Stodare, Colonel (Jack English or Alfred Inglis, 1831–66). British magician notable for his dramatic presentations of the *Basket Trick* and the *Sphinx*. There is a good deal of uncertainty about his real name. In his early years he was an itinerant sign-painter and travelling conjurer, but later, under his assumed name, he performed regularly at the *Egyptian Hall*, London. Had he not died at 35 he might have become one of the great magicians of his day. His book of magical instruction, *FLY-NOTES* (1867) was far in advance of its time. See Lamb, *VICTORIAN MAGIC*, pp.67–9.

Stodare egg. *egg, hollow.*

stooge. *confederate.*

strait-jacket escape. Form of escapology originated and popularized by *Houdini*. The jacket is a form of restraint for violent lunatics, having

137

long sleeves terminating in straps which fasten behind the lunatic's back, binding his arms across the front of his body. The key to escaping is to get comparative freedom for the arms by forcing them over the head. Houdini (followed by a number of later escapers) made the act sensational by freeing himself while suspended upside down from a tall crane or high building; *illustration 63*. See Gibson, *HOUDINI'S ESCAPES*, pp.45–7; Cannell, *THE SECRETS OF HOUDINI*, pp.157–60.

string, cut and restored. A long piece of string is held by both ends in one hand while the performer's other hand lifts up the middle of the hanging loop and apparently presents it in both hands for cutting by a spectator. In fact at the right moment the middle is secretly dropped and a part near one end caught up and presented instead; *illustration 136*. The string is then restored by being wound round one hand, the short piece cut off being palmed. Another (Elizabethan) method 'to cut a lace (cord) asunder in the middest' was to have a small extra piece secretly palmed and to present this for cutting. There are several variations of method and material. See Gibson, *HOUDINI'S MAGIC*, pp.15–16, *PROFESSIONAL MAGIC FOR AMATEURS*, pp.139–42; Rawson, *COLOUR BOOK OF MAGIC*, p.30; Cannell, *100 BEST TRICKS*, pp.148–9.

stripper pack. Cards which are slightly narrower at one end than at the other. If a chosen card is replaced in a pack which has all the other cards the opposite way up, it can easily be found by touch and 'stripped out' from the pack. Also known as *biseauté* pack.

Substitution Trunk. Popular stage illusion with which *Houdini* first made his name. An assistant is placed in a sack and locked inside a trunk, which is then securely roped. The performer stands on the trunk, holding a large cloth in front of himself. He begins counting up to three or four, and on the last count the cloth is dropped, revealing the assistant. The trunk is unroped and unlocked, and the performer is found within the sack. The secret is a hinged panel in the trunk, considerable agility, and perfect timing. See Page, *BIG BOOK OF MAGIC*, pp.268–71.

sucker trick (or gag). Trick (or dodge)

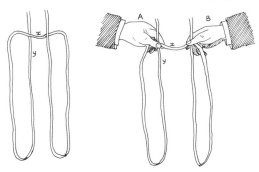

136. Cut and Restored String. The string at *x* is surreptitiously dropped by hand B and seized at *y* instead.

137. A sucker trick.

for making the audience believe that the performer has made a slip, only to reveal, after some byplay, that he has been fooling them; *illustration 137. sliding die box.*

Sun and Moon Trick. A white handkerchief and a coloured one have a piece cut from the centre of each. The conjurer then proposes to restore the damage, but finds that the coloured centre has gone to the white handkerchief and vice versa. Eventually both handkerchiefs are restored to their proper condition.

Sunshade Trick. Old *transposition* trick in which a bright sunshade is shown and then wrapped up in a sheet of paper or a mat. Some *silks* are placed in a *cone* or other container and a magic *pass* is made. The sunshade is withdrawn from the paper with silks attached to its ribs, while the cover has transferred itself to the cone. After another pass things are brought back to normal. The main secret is an extra sunshade concealed in a hidden pocket of the paper. An ingenious device invented and patented by *Lewis Davenport* enabled the paper to be bundled up after the trick, seemingly showing that only one sunshade was used. The trick is also known as the Mutilated Parasol.

138. Supreme Magic Company building at Bideford.

139

Supreme Magic Co. Magic firm founded by *Hooper* (Edwin) in 1953 in one room of a house in the small Devonshire town of Bideford. Since then it has grown into one of the largest magic dealers in the world, employing over a dozen full-time distributive workers and a large number of out-worker specialist makers of apparatus. It has over 20,000 customers on its books and about 10,000 tricks and gadgets on its shelves. Roughly 75 per cent of the goods are exported all over the world, particularly the U.S.A. As well as dealing in tricks Supreme is a leading magical publisher, with over 400 books and booklets in its list; it also publishes *MAGIGRAM* and *NEW PENTAGRAM*. Edwin's right-hand man is Ian Adair, prolific author and inventor, together with Edwin's son, Michael. The firm occupies a large building (No. 64) in Bideford High Street; *illustration 138*.

Svengali pack. Forcing pack of cards, deriving its name from a notorious hypnotist in the late-Victorian novel *TRILBY*. It consists of 26 short cards, all alike, and 26 ordinary cards, all different. Short and ordinary cards alternate, with a short at the top. When the pack is *riffled* only the ordinary cards are seen, but if a spectator inserts a finger during the riffle it will always rest on a short card. See Gibson, *COMPLETE ILLUSTRATED BOOK OF CARD MAGIC*, pp.357–61; Jean Hugard, *ENCYCLOPEDIA OF CARD TRICKS*, pp.272–83.

Swami gimmick. Small *thumb-writer* or nail-writer. 'Swami' is really a term of respect used by Hindus, particularly in addressing a religious leader.

switch. Exchange one article for another without the audience seeing the manoeuvre.

switch-box. Small box (e.g. chocolate box) for *forcing* a name which has been previously written on several folded *billets* inside the box. Spectators are invited to write names of their choice on billets, then to fold them and put them through a slit in the lid of the box. They really go into a secret compartment attached to the lid. When the latter is removed, any billet picked from the box must be a forced one. See also Severn, *MAGIC WITH PAPER*, pp.125–8.

sword, card on. *card sword.*

sword cabinet. A girl enters a cabinet in which numerous swords are then thrust at various angles through slots in the side. When the door is opened she appears to have vanished, and when the swords are withdrawn she reappears unhurt. The *mirror principle* is employed. A mirror (face inward) lies against each side of the cabinet. Pulled open, the two meet at an angle, the join being hidden by a sword which is thrust straight down from the top. *Proteus cabinet.*

symbol, magic. *rabbit.*

Sympathetic Silks. Favourite trick with handkerchiefs. Six *silks* are shown apparently separate. Three are laid aside; the other three are knotted together. The knots are waved towards the separate silks, which are now discovered to have become knotted. The reverse process now takes place, the unknotting of one set of silks resulting in the mysterious unknotting of the others. The secret lies in false counting the silks to start with, three of them being in fact already knotted. Afterwards false knots are tied, which dissolve when the silks are sharply pulled. See Hugard, *MODERN MAGIC MANUAL*, pp.194–9.

T

table. The days have long departed when the conjurer had a large table full of traps, with a cloth reaching to the floor concealing an assistant. Some years ago a *black art* table used to be popular, with *wells* (for vanishing articles) disguised by geometrical patterns on the table-top, but this is now rather old-fashioned. A common form of table has long been the kind with a music-stand type of base, useful for portability, either bought from a dealer or self-made (see Tuffs, *TEACH YOURSELF CONJURING*, pp.129–32). For a simple *close-up* or party performance a card table covered with a neat cloth is quite adequate. Some dealers supply a

139–140. Cane and top hat as a table.

table which can be turned into a suitcase in which the legs and a certain amount of apparatus can be carried. Comedy conjurers sometimes use a joke table whose front legs fall off when it is lifted, being replaced automatically by supports resembling a lady's legs. A clever little table for the sleight-of-hand performer is formed from a cane and top hat, into which cards or coins can be dropped as they are produced at the fingertips; *illustrations 139, 140. servante.*

talking. Applied to an object making a sound that betrays its secret presence: e.g. a palmed coin chinking against another, or an article within a supposedly empty container knocking against the side of it.

Talking Hand. *Rapping Hand.*

tambourine. For conjuring purposes a piece of apparatus for the production of a *coil* and other articles. It is constructed during the performance, and consists of two metal rings between which a sheet of thin paper is pressed, the superfluous paper being trimmed away. A coil hidden on the table or on a *servante* is secretly picked up, a hole is made in the tambourine, and the coil pulled through rapidly; *illustration 141*. Under cover of the bunched-up ᴄᴏⁱˡ ᴏᵗʰᵉʳ ᴀʳᵗⁱᶜˡᵉˢ ᴄᴀɴ ᵗʰᵉⁿ ᵇᵉ ᵖʳᵒduced from a servante or elsewhere.

Tarbell cone. *cone; illustration 49.*

Tarbell Course in Magic. An immensely comprehensive attempt by an experienced American magician, Harlan Tarbell (1890–1960), to teach magic scientifically and

141

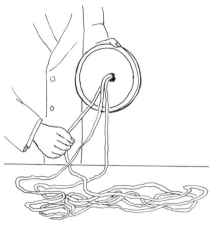

141. Tambourine for coil production.

exhaustively. It began in 1926 as a series of 60 lessons sent regularly to subscribers. Some years later the original lessons, partly rearranged and considerably added to, began to be published in volume form (1941–54), most of them edited by R. W. Read. There were six volumes: much later a seventh was added (1972, ed. H. Lorayne). Altogether they form a kind of encyclopedia of about 3,000 pages. They contain a vast amount of useful and reliable information on all kinds of tricks, but are more likely to be of value to the reasonably experienced magician than to the beginner, who is not best served by being given enormous numbers of sleights to practise, or being shown numerous ways of producing the same effect.

Taylor, Harold. Lively, versatile, and widely travelled professional magician who has given thousands of shows to audiences large and small, with the accent on comedy and entertainment. Experienced also as a musician, compère, lecturer, and

actor. In earlier years a performer at the *Windmill Theatre*.

telepathy. *ESP.*

telephone trick. Usually a chosen card is revealed over the telephone by the magician's accomplice to a spectator who rings him up during the performance. The commonest method is the use of a secret code by which the accomplice's supposed name indicates the card: e.g. Alan = Ace Clubs, Albert = Ace Diamonds, and so on. An alternative and simpler plan is to force the card, the identity of which is already known to the accomplice. Telephone tricks are apt to be more ingenious than entertaining, and the circumstances in which they can be used are limited.

Ten Ichi ('The Heavenly One'). The father of modern Japanese magic, who gave his name to the popular *Thumb Tie*, and who also produced a spectacular closing illusion (copied by *Thurston* and *Dante*) with fountains of water spurting from everything and everyone touched by his wand. Another Ten Ichi toured the U.S.A. from 1901 to 1905 and then returned to Japan. A Ten Ichi troupe (three women and a man) performed in Europe c.1908. A Dutch family of magicians also adopted the name and nationality of Ten Ichi.

thick card. Double card formed by sticking two cards together; used as a *locator card*. A dab of wax or moisture can be used for an impromptu thick card.

thimble manipulation. Thimbles are fairly easy to manipulate as they fit nicely on a fingertip and are comfortably held in a *thumb-palm* position. To vanish a thimble, place it on the right forefinger, apparently grasp it in the left hand, but actually thumb-palm it as soon as it is hidden

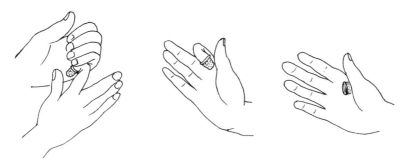

142. Thimble manipulation. Thimble on right forefinger apparently grasped in left hand but really thumb-palmed in right.

by the left fingers; *illustration 142*. Pull the forefinger out of the fist as though leaving the thimble within. In due course show the left hand empty, and then reproduce the thimble from (say) behind the left elbow. Many variations are possible, and a whole *thimble* routine may be presented, particularly suitable, perhaps, for *magiciennes*. See Hugard, *MODERN MAGIC MANUAL*, pp.244–60; Robinson, *MAGIC AS A PASTIME*, pp.41–4; Delvin, *MAGIC OF THE MASTERS*, pp.164–75.

Thimble Rig. Form of *Three-card Trick* with thimbles and a pea.

Thirty-card Trick. *Cards Across.*

thought-reading. *mentalism.*

thread. Often said to be the conjurer's best friend. Black thread is commonly used, though dark brown may be even more invisible against a dark background. A long human hair is even harder to see, though not so strong. Some performers swear by very fine fishing-line. Tricks such as the *Rising Cards*, *Floating Ball*, *Rapping Hand*, *Dancing Cane*, etc., are examples of its use. Thread bought from a magic dealer is likely to be the most reliable for conjuring.

Three-card Trick. A favourite with street and race-course tricksters, and often known as 'Find the Lady'. Three cards are shown, the centre one being a Queen (though a Jack or Ace is often used instead). They are dropped face down on whatever is being used as a table, and the victim is invited to bet on which is the lady. The centre one seems obvious, but an adroit move as the cards are dropped puts one of the others in the centre; whichever the victim chooses, in fact, he may still lose the bet (*Mexican turnover*). Conjurers perform this as a close-up trick, sometimes using sleight-of-hand, sometimes simpler methods. See Baron, *CARD TRICKS FOR BEGINNERS*, pp.46, 78, 83.

Three-ring Routine. Version of the *Linking Rings* using only the key ring and two others; the linking and unlinking are usually performed very deliberately.

throw a card. To hold a card between the fingers and flick it forward so that it sails into the audience, sometimes returning to the performer. *Thurston* was a master of the art. See Thurston, *CARD TRICKS*, pp.8, 69–70; Hoffmann, *MODERN MAGIC*, pp.38–9; Hugard and Braue, *ROYAL ROAD TO CARD*

MAGIC, pp.60–1; Stanyon, *CONJUR-ING WITH CARDS*, pp.15–17.

thumb palm. Concealment of a small article usually in the fork of the thumb; *illustrations 43, 142*. With a coin an additional form of thumb palm is concealment in the crook of the thumb.

Thumb Tie. Possibly Japanese in origin, but it has been freely used by Western conjurers, and was known to *Pinetti*. The performer places his thumbs together, crossed, and invites a spectator to tie them vertically and horizontally (*illustration 143*), using stiff or stiffened cord, or sometimes pipe-cleaners. Despite this he is able to catch on his arms several large rings thrown to him. He deftly slips one thumb from the tie at the critical moment, and because the loop is stiff it remains open for him to replace his thumb instantly. The trick is effective but needs a good deal of address and perfect timing. *Ten Ichi.*

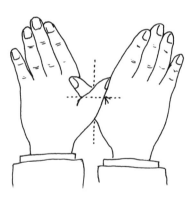

143. Thumb Tie. Dotted lines show where thumbs are tied.

thumb tip. Metal or plastic *gimmick*, usually flesh-coloured, fitting over the tip of the thumb. It is just large enough to hold a duplicate strip for the *torn and restored paper*, or a small *silk*, or even half a lighted cigarette. The last is vanished by being pushed apparently into the left fist, which conceals the tip, and this is then removed on the right thumb. The tip can be used for either producing or vanishing a silk. See Robinson, *MAGIC AS A PAS-TIME*, pp.57–60; Page, *BIG BOOK OF MAGIC*, pp.169–71.

thumb-writer. *Gimmick* that fits over the tip of the thumb and has a pencil point attached. It is often used for secretly writing a supposed *predic-tion*. The performer pretends to write his prediction on a card, and then, when told the chosen name or number, surreptitiously scribbles it with the thumb-writer. *nail-writer.* See Corinda, *13 STEPS TO MENTAL-ISM*, pp.4–24.

Thurston, Howard (1869–1936). Famous American magician who began his career as 'The King of Cards'. After a successful European and Eastern tour lasting several years, his big moment came in 1908 when *Kellar* agreed to accept him as his successor. Thurston now became America's leading magician, presenting large-scale illusions in a very impressive way. He brought Kellar's show up to date by using a bevy of attractive girls as assistants and by vanishing a motor car. One of his most striking illusions was Iasia, the disappearance of a girl from a cabinet suspended high above the auditorium. He died shortly after suffering from a stroke during a farewell tour of America. Most of the books published under his name were written by *Walter Gibson*, at one time on his staff.

top card. Card at the top of a face-down pack. *bottom card.*

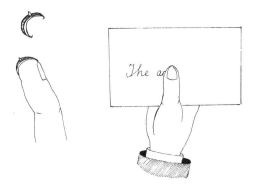

144. Thumb writer or nail writer.

Topit vanisher. Dark cloth bag fastened between the trousers waistband and inside jacket, for receiving vanished articles.

Torn and Restored Paper. Very popular trick presented in many forms. In its simplest, a long strip of paper is shown and deliberately torn into a number of pieces, which are rolled into a ball and then opened out restored to a long strip. A duplicate strip is *finger-palmed* and *switched* for the torn pieces, or a *thumb tip* may be used for the switching. A cigarette paper or a sheet of tissue or newspaper sometimes replaces the long strip. *Oswald Williams* used to offer his audiences a choice of colour. *Lyle* added *transformation* to restoration, the torn sheet of tissue being restored in the form of a paper hat. A common embellishment is to repeat the trick under the pretence of showing how it is done. See Hay, *AMATEUR MAGICIAN'S HANDBOOK*, pp.232–4; Baron, *MAGIC SIMPLIFIED*, pp.37–40; Delvin, *MAGIC OF THE MASTERS*, p.180.

torn corner. A feature of tricks in which a chosen card is torn up or burnt is that one corner of the card is usually retained by a spectator. When the torn card is 'restored' there is a piece missing, which the retained corner exactly fits. In fact the 'restored' card is a duplicate, and its torn-off corner was switched for the corner of the original card.

Torrini. According to *Robert-Houdin's MEMOIRS*, a travelling magician who saved him from a serious illness when he was young, and who also helped him to develop his conjuring skill. Torrini was stated to be really the Comte de Grisy, who had formerly been a bitter rival of *Pinetti*. The story of Torrini has been frequently repeated in histories of magic, but his existence is questionable. There appear to be no records whatever of his career, and it is highly probable that Robert-Houdin was romanticizing. It is quite likely that the rivalry with Pinetti was suggested by Decremps' feud with the Italian.

tourniquet. *French drop.*

transfer. There are two kinds of transfer in magic: *actual* (the passing of an article from one hand to the other), and *apparent* (*simulation* of actual transfer, the article being retained in the original hand).

145

Apparent transfer should copy as closely as possible the exact movements of actual transfer.

transformation. The act of apparently changing an article into something different in shape, size, colour, or identity, as with the *Diminishing Cards* or *colour-changing silk*, or the apparent changing of one person into another (*Metempsychosis*).

transposition. Making articles or persons apparently change places with each other; e.g. *Bottle and Glass Trick*; *Substitution Trunk*.

trick. The *SHORTER OXFORD DICTIONARY* gives as one of its definitions: 'a feat of dexterity or skill intended to surprise or amuse'. This is the sense in which the word is commonly understood both by the general public and by most magicians. Thus we quite naturally speak of the *Indian Rope Trick* and the *Basket Trick*. The efforts of some magical theorists to ban the word 'trick' and substitute a supposedly more dignified word (e.g. 'experiment') have had little success and are quite unnecessary. For 'trick' in the narrower sense of 'cunning device' most conjurers use the term 'secret'.

Trouble Wit. Paper folding with a special type of pleated paper, a speciality of *Ellis Stanyon*, described in his *CONJURING FOR AMATEURS*, pp.108–15, and in Lang Neil, *THE MODERN CONJURER*, pp.353–70.

trouser-pocket dodge. If a small article is placed at the top of the trouser-pocket it will not be seen when the rest of the pocket is pulled out and shown empty. *Cards to Pocket.*

turnover. Term used in several ways in card magic. (1) It is sometimes necessary to turn the pack over secretly, either to bring it face up or, when it has been *boxed*, to bring the under half uppermost. This can be done by placing the thumb under the pack and pressing upward, so that the pack swivels over, under cover of the other hand; *illustration 145*. (2) When the pack has been *ribbon spread*, if a finger is placed under the card at the farthest end and pressed gently and firmly upward, all the cards in the spread will gradually turn over and become reversed. (3) *Mexican turnover.*

Twentieth Century Silks. Popular (rather overworked) handkerchief

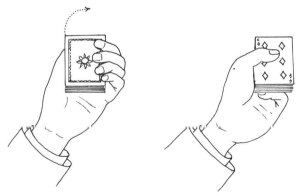

145. The turnover, showing face down pack swivelled face up.

trick. Three *silks* are shown, two of which (e.g. blue) are placed in a hat or other container. The third (e.g. red) is now vanished, and is subsequently found tied between the two blue. Methods vary, but there is usually a duplicate red silk already knotted to the two blue, but cunningly concealed. One form of up-dating lies in making the performer's sock appear between the blue silks, the red handkerchief being found tied round his ankle in place of the missing sock. His girl assistant's stocking, etc., may be used instead of his own sock.

two-person telepathy. Form of *mentalism* in which the performer works with a partner or *medium*, who appears to read his mind. Often the performer receives various articles from members of the audience and 'mentally' conveys information about these to the medium. Cards, numbers, and words may be similarly conveyed, a *code* of some kind being used in all cases. *one-man mentalism.*

U

undercut. With the cards in the hands, to draw out the lower half and place it on top of the pack. *cut, false.*

Unequal Equal Ropes. Three pieces of rope are shown to be of different sizes. Taking them by the ends, the performer pulls them to show that they have now become equal. Then he reveals that they have become unequal again. Smoothly performed, and supported with a good story line, the trick (worked by sleight-of-hand) is most convincing and effective. Sometimes known by other titles; e.g. Equally Unequal Ropes.

unloading. Removing a *load* (especially *body load*) from its place of concealment to the place from which it is to be *produced.*

'Unmasking of Robert-Houdin'. Book (1906) by *Houdini*, purporting to expose the deficiencies of his former hero, *Robert-Houdin*, long after his death. Contains useful historical material, much of it coming from playbills bought from an impoverished collector; but its unbalanced and unpleasant bias (partly inspired by a rebuff from the Frenchman's widowed daughter-in-law) robs it of any claim to be a genuine history. Its literary style probably owes something to a ghost writer. See Sardinia, *WHERE HOUDINI WAS WRONG* (1950), a justified defence, though sometimes a little wild.

upside-down card. *reversed card.*

146. Typical mid-Victorian magician's stage setting. ('Magic', March 1905.)

V

vanish. Cause to disappear. Although 'vanish' is normally an intransitive verb, conjurers far more often use it transitively, vanishing a card, coin, ball, lady, etc.

Vanishing Cane. A cane or walking-stick disappears, or changes to a handkerchief, either when held in the hand or when wrapped in paper. Though it looks like an ordinary cane, it is in fact a coiled spring, compressing rapidly when required into a size small enough to be palmed. Obtainable from dealers. See Page, *THE BIG BOOK OF MAGIC*, pp.247–50.

Vanishing Lady. Perhaps the most famous of all stage illusions, invented by *De Kolta* and first presented by him in Paris in 1886.

The magician spread a newspaper on the floor, placed a chair on it, invited a young lady *assistant* to sit on it, and covered her and the chair with a large cloth. A moment later he snatched the cloth away, revealing that the lady had completely disappeared. In due course she reappeared from the wings. In some later versions the cloth also vanished as it was seized. In spite of appearances the lady vanished through a trap in the stage, there being a trap in the newspaper also, and the seat of the chair being made to swivel downward. Wire shapes, cunningly concealed, were pulled from the chair to represent her head and knees while she was escaping. The trick caused a sensation; later it was widely copied, legitimately by *Bertram*, illicitly (and often badly) by many other performers. It is rarely seen today. See Dexter, THIS IS MAGIC, pp.53–6.

Vanishing Wand. Popular opening trick performed in various ways. Often the wand is first tapped hard on the table to show its solidity, then inserted in a long envelope, which is suddenly crushed into a ball, showing that the wand has vanished. It may be reproduced from another envelope or from the performer's jacket. The wand inserted in the envelope is in fact a *shell* with a small piece of wood or ivorine at one end. See Hugard, MODERN MAGIC MANUAL, pp.21–3.

Vase, Lota. *Lota Vase.*

Vernon, Dai (David Werner). Generally regarded by the conjuring fraternity as the supreme magical artist of the day. Born (of remote Irish descent) and brought up in Canada, he has lived for a great many years in the U.S.A., at one time earning his living by cutting silhouettes. Though he occasionally appeared (successfully) on the stage, he has always been essentially a close-up performer, and his artistry and passion for perfection have made him an important influence on this branch of magic. Many of his ideas have been admirably written up by *Lewis Ganson*, in THE DAI VERNON BOOK OF MAGIC (1957), DAI VERNON'S ULTIMATE CARD SECRETS (1967), and other books. *Illustration 147.*

Victor, Edward (1885–1964). Notable British *sleight-of-hand* performer (of Swiss parentage), who made a great reputation in music halls and at Maskelyne's *St George's Hall*. His hands were remarkable, not only in magical manipulations of

147. The Dai Vernon Book of Magic.

cards, billiard balls, and thimbles, but also in expert shadowgraphy. His books, MAGIC OF THE HANDS (1937) and two sequels, are sleight-of-hand classics.

Victorian Magic. The Victorian period saw the rise of the magician as a respected figure in English society. At the beginning of the nineteenth century the conjurer was still very much a fairground performer. By 1900 he was often a distinguished figure, on friendly terms with royalty and the nobility. Performances were frequently given on the stages of great theatres, and stage settings were often lavish and elaborate: *illustration 146*. Among the great Victorian magicians were *Anderson, Stodare, Maskelyne,* *Lynn, De Kolta, Morritt,* and *Bertram*. See Lamb, *VICTORIAN MAGIC.*

W

Wade, John. Accomplished British magician who developed his professional skill at the *Windmill Theatre*, among other places. He has performed often for TV and was at one time magical adviser for a *David Nixon* series. In 1977 he successfully played the name part in *THE MAGIC MAN* at a London theatre. He is an experienced cruise entertainer and an expert compère. His book *THE TRADE OF THE TRICKS* (1974) gives a lively account of his professional career and of the modern magic scene.

Walking through a Brick Wall. Famous stage illusion probably originated by *Selbit*. A carpet is spread in the middle of the stage to indicate the absence of traps. A brick wall erected on a very low wheeled base is examined by a committee of spectators and pushed into the centre of the carpet. The performer (or an assistant) stands close to one side of the wall; screens are placed around him and on the opposite side of the wall, while the committee stand all around. After a few seconds the screens are removed; he/she is now standing on the other side of the wall. The secret is really simple. In spite of the carpet a trap *is* used, allowing the carpet to sag just enough for a person to crawl under the wall. See Gibson, *PROFESSIONAL MAGIC FOR AMATEURS*, pp.205–8.

wand. Magician's symbol of mystic power, used by Aaron (*EXODUS*, vii), by the ancient Egyptians, by the Druids, and by medieval wizards. Victorian magicians made great play with it. The wand is less employed today, but it remains useful. Because of its long history most audiences accept it as a matter of course. Handling it can disguise the *stealing* or releasing of an article, and can assist palming. The wand may be used as a piece of apparatus in its own right, to be vanished or magnetized; it can also be *faked* to help in some trick (e.g. *coin wand*, *handkerchief wand*), or used for comedy (e.g. *breakaway wand*). See Hugard, *MODERN MAGIC MANUAL*, pp.19–23; Hoffmann, *LATER MAGIC*, pp.102–33.

Warlock, Peter (Alec Bell). One of the most active and knowledgeable men in magic as author, editor, lecturer, inventor, performer, and magical historian. Covers a wide field but specializes in *mentalism*; has presented many subtle ideas both in

148. Houdini's Water Torture Cell: a typical Houdini poster.

magical journals and in books. Editor of *PENTAGRAM* and *NEW PENTAGRAM*; author of *THE COMPLETE BOOK OF MAGIC* (1956), *THE BEST TRICKS WITH SLATES* (1942), *WARLOCK'S WAY* (1966), and several other books. Until retirement a bank official.

Water Torture Cell. *Houdini*'s most notable escape trick, first presented in 1912. A glass-fronted tank nearly six feet high and three feet square was filled with water on the stage. Houdini was locked into this upside down, with only his feet protruding through the fastened lid; *illustration 148*. A screen was pushed in front, and two attendants stood by with axes ready. Two long minutes would elapse; then, just as the men seemed about to dash to the rescue, Houdini would stagger from behind the screen. *Howard Peters* has repeated the feat in recent times.

wax, magician's. Type of wax which sticks articles together but does not leave a mark when removed; obtainable from dealers. Blu-tack can also be used.

well. *Black Art.*

Westcar Papyrus. Important document in magical history, recording the first known conjuring performance, that of *Dedi*. The papyrus dates from about 1700 B.C., but Dedi's performance apparently took place about 1,000 years earlier. The papyrus was probably discovered by natives in an Egyptian tomb at the beginning of the nineteenth century and was acquired by Henry Westcar, a British Egyptologist, about 1823. Its subsequent history is blurred. It somehow came into the possession of a German Egyptologist, was later in Berlin State Museum (1884–1939), and is believed to be now in a Russian museum.

Where Do the Ducks Go? Stage illusion typical of the kind popular with some magicians several years ago. Two or three ducks in an openwork basket are removed and placed in a box resting on a small table. The box is then taken to pieces without a sign of the ducks; and although the spectators are led to believe they are concealed in the table, this is shown to be just a *sucker* gag. The mysterious secret lies in the cramming of the birds into a narrow bag attached to the inside of the lid, which is casually placed on top of the basket while the audience's suspicion is being attracted to the table. Fortunately the trick is not often seen today. *Illustration 149.*

White, Francis. A distinguished figure in magic, secretary of the *Magic Circle* for many years and president since 1958.

wild card. Playing-card which apparently causes other cards to change to its own suit and value.

'Will, the Witch, and the Watch'. The most famous magical sketch ever devised, presented by *J. N. Maskelyne* at his two *Homes of Mystery* over 11,000 times. Intended largely as a vehicle for the *Box Trick* and Maskelyne's own version of the *Cabinet of Proteus*. The cabinet was used as a lock-up into which the watchman thrust a handsome sailor. His sweetheart, together with a witch, a monkey, and the watchman's companion also came into the action, during which the various characters kept appearing in and disappearing from the lock-up with a frequency that left the audience (and the committee on the stage) utterly bewildered. A large part of the secret lay in the changing of costumes and hiding of persons within

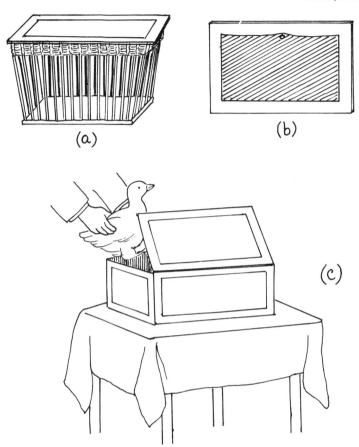

149. Where Do the Ducks Go? Showing (a) basket, (b) lid with bag attached, and (c) insertion of duck.

the cabinet. See Jasper Maskelyne, *WHITE MAGIC*, pp.30–63.

Williams, Oswald (1881–1937). Clever and inventive British illusionist who established a reputation in music halls and for a while became the main performer at *St George's Hall* after *Devant* had left

Maskelyne's. Effective though his presentations were, he lacked the easy charm of his famous predecessor. *Dizzy Limit*.

Wilson, Mark. American magician who has made a great reputation mainly with TV and trade shows, after studying advertising as a young

153

man. His *MARK WILSON COURSE IN MAGIC* (1976) is expensive but forms a comprehensive guide to almost every aspect of conjuring. About a third is devoted to card tricks.

Windmill Theatre. London variety theatre (1931–64) noted for the stationary nudity of its girls and for remaining open throughout the last war, despite air raids. ('We never closed!') Notable magically as a nursery for several subsequently distinguished conjurers, including *Nixon*, *Berglas*, Tommy Cooper, *Johnson*, *Taylor*, and *Wade*.

woofle dust. Imaginary magic powder

'used' by many conjurers, ostensibly to sprinkle on an object to make it vanish or change but actually as a not very subtle excuse for the conjurer to put his hand in his pocket to dispose of a palmed object. *misdirection*.

words, magic. *magic words.*

wrist chopper. Apparatus in the form of a small guillotine for apparently cutting off a volunteer's hand at the wrist; *illustration 41*. The presentation is almost invariably humorous, sometimes with a dummy hand allowed to fall into a bucket below the blade. *chopper effects*.

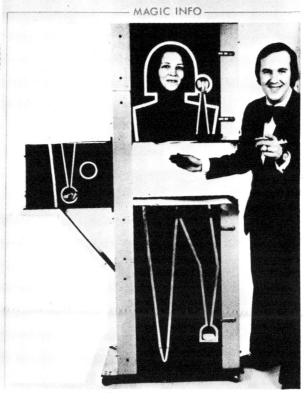

MAGIC INFO

150. The Zig-Zag Girl, presented by a Finnish magician.

Z

Zancigs, The. The most famous of all stage telepathic performers, who publicized themselves as 'Two Minds with but a Single Thought'. Julius Zancig was a Dane who emigrated to America, married a childhood friend, and developed with her a complicated *code* which they used with incredible speed. He published his code in a British weekly journal in 1924. When his first wife died he later worked up his act with a second wife. He himself died in 1929.

Zig-Zag Girl. *Harbin*; *illustration 150.*

Zodiac. An imaginary circular zone of sky representing the path taken by the sun, as worked out by the ancient Babylonians. Freely used in astrology. The Zodiac circle is the symbol of the *Magic Circle*. The signs can sometimes be introduced into conjuring to give colour and add piquancy. Starting at Aries (*illustration 151*) and moving clockwise, they represent respectively: Ram, Bull, Twins, Crab, Lion, Virgin, Scales, Scorpion, Archer, Goat, Water-bearer, Fishes.

Zombie. Form of *Floating Ball* worked not with thread but with a thin wire *gimmick* attached to the finger. Effective when well presented. A zombie is really a West Indian term for a dead body supposed to have been brought back to life in order to work.

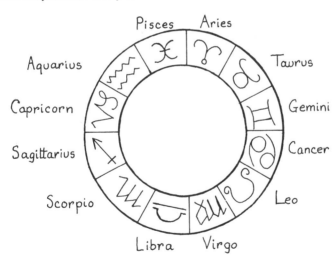

151. The Zodiac Circle.

SOME MAGIC BOOKS FOR BEGINNERS

ADAIR, IAN: Conjuring as a Craft; David & Charles, 1970.

ANDERSON, GEORGE: Magic Digest; Digest Books, Illinois, 1972.

BARON, HARRY: Better Magic; Kaye & Ward, 1978.
  Card Tricks for Beginners; Kaye & Ward, 1969.
  Close-up Magic for Beginners; Kaye & Ward, 1972.
  Magic for Beginners; Kaye & Ward, 1967.

CLIVE, PAUL: Card Tricks Without Skill; Faber, 1959. (Good, though the title is misleading.)

DELVIN, JACK: Magic of the Masters; Hamlyn, 1977.

DEXTER, WILL: 101 Magic Secrets; Arco, 1957.

ELLIOTT, BRUCE: Classic Secrets of Magic; Faber, 1953.
  Magic as a Hobby: Faber, 1951.
  Magic – 100 New Tricks; Faber, 1957.

FISHER, JOHN: John Fisher's Magic Book; Muller, 1968.

HAY, HENRY: Amateur Magician's Handbook; Faber, 1971 (reprint).

HUGARD, JEAN: Modern Magic Manual; Faber, 1957.

KAYE, MARVIN: The Complete Magician; Macmillan, 1974.

LAMB, GEOFFREY: Your Book of Card Tricks; Faber, 1972.
  Your Book of Mental Magic; Faber, 1973.
  Your Book of Table Tricks; Faber, 1974.

REED, GRAHAM: Magic for Every Occasion; Kaye & Ward, 1978.
  Magical Miracles You Can Do; Kaye & Ward, 1977.

ROBINSON, GEOFFREY: Magic as a Pastime; Souvenir Press, 1960.

SCARNE, JOHN: Scarne on Card Tricks; Constable, 1970 (reprint).

SEVERN, BILL: Magic from Your Pocket; Faber, 1965.

SOME STANDARD MAGIC BOOKS

CHRISTOPHER, MILBOURNE: Illustrated History of Magic; Hale, 1975.

CORINDA, TONY: 13 Steps to Mentalism; Clarke, 1960.

DEVANT, DAVID: The Best Tricks; Pearson, 1931.
Secrets of My Magic, Hutchinson, 1936; Supreme, 1971.

EVANS, H. R.: The Old Magic and the New; Kegan, Paul, 1909.

GARDNER, MARTIN: Mathematics, Magic, & Mystery; Dover, 1956.

GANSON, LEWIS: Dai Vernon Book of Magic; Unique, 1957, Supreme, 1971.

GIBSON, WALTER: Complete Illustrated Book of Card Magic; Kaye & Ward, 1969.

HILLIARD, J. N.: Greater Magic; C. W. Jones, 1938.

HOFFMANN, PROFESSOR: Modern Magic; Routledge, 1876 (many editions).
More Magic; Routledge, 1890.
Later Magic; Routledge, 1904, 1951.

HUGARD, JEAN: Encyclopedia of Card Tricks; Faber, 1937, 1961.

HUGARD & BRAUE: Royal Road to Card Magic; Faber, 1949.

LAMB, GEOFFREY: Victorian Magic; Routledge, 1976.

MASKELYNE & DEVANT: Our Magic; Routledge, 1911; Supreme, 1971.

NEIL, C. LANG: The Modern Conjurer; Pearson, 1903; Kemp, 1937.

PAGE, PATRICK: The Big Book of Magic; Wolfe, 1976.

ROBERT-HOUDIN, J. E.: Secrets of Conjuring & Magic; Routledge, 1878.

SACHS, E. T.: Sleight of Hand; Upcott Gill, 1877.

TARBELL, HARLAN: The Tarbell Course in Magic; Tanner, 1941–72.
See also bibliographies, conjuring; history of magic.